TEN GOLDEN KEYS TO YOUR ABUNDANCE

Rod Parsley

RESULTS
PUBLISHING

Columbus, Ohio

Unless otherwise indicated, all Scripture quotations
are taken from the *King James Version* of the Bible.

TEN GOLDEN KEYS TO YOUR ABUNDANCE

ISBN: 1-880244-20-9
Copyright © 1995 by Rod Parsley.

Published by:
Results Publishing
Box 32932
Columbus, Ohio 43232-0932 USA

ABOUT THE AUTHOR

Rod Parsley began his ministry as an energetic 19 year old, in the backyard of his parents' Ohio home. The fresh, "old-time Gospel" approach of Parsley's delivery immediately attracted a hungry God-seeking audience. From the 17 people who attended the first backyard meeting, the crowds grew rapidly.

Today, as the pastor of Columbus, Ohio's, 5200-seat World Harvest Church, Parsley oversees World Harvest's preschool-12 Christian Academy; World Harvest Bible College; numerous church-sponsored outreaches; and Breakthrough, World Harvest Church's daily and weekly television broadcast, currently available to 96% of the population of the United States and parts of Canada.

Rod Parsley also serves as Dr. Lester Sumrall's personal assistant in directing the End-Time Joseph "Feed the Hungry" program.

To contact the author write:

Rod Parsley
Breakthrough
P.O. Box 32932
Columbus, Ohio 43232-0932
24 Hour Prayer Line: (614) 837-3232
TDD: (614) 327-8337

CONTENTS

Introduction: THE REVELATION OF GOD'S   7
    ABUNDANCE

Golden Key #1: THE PROCESS OF EXCHANGE   29

Golden Key #2: THE PROCESS OF POSSESSION 49
    (Going to War)

Golden Key #3: THE PROCESS OF   69
    PROTECTING YOUR SEED

Golden Key #4: THE PROCESS OF   87
    WATERING YOUR SEED

Golden Key #5: THE PROCESS OF   107
    SELECTING YOUR SOIL

Golden Key #6: TAKE YOUR OFFERING   123
    TO THE PRIEST

Golden Key #7: MIRACLE WORKING POWER 137
    OF THE SANCTIFIED SEED

Golden Key #8: SOW YOUR SEED IN TIME 149
    OF FAMINE

Golden Key #9: UNCLEAN SEED   159

Golden Key #10: GOD CAN'T BLESS   169
    WHAT HE'S CURSED

IT'S TIME TO OPEN THE DOOR   179

INTRODUCTION

THE REVELATION OF GOD'S ABUNDANCE

You'll never know how thrilled I am that you are holding this book in your hands. Why? Because I know in advance what is about to happen.

What you are on the verge of discovering is greater than all of the gold in Fort Knox and more valuable than hidden diamonds in the mines of South Africa.

These keys of abundance were not found by accident. I didn't just happen to be walking down a street in Columbus, Ohio, and exclaim, "Wow! Look at those golden keys! I wonder what they are for."

No. The treasure I possess is the result of a twenty year spiritual journey that has totally transformed my life.

It took God ten years just to bring me to the point where He could *begin* to release this revelation into my spirit. It wasn't ten weeks, or ten months, but a *decade* of divine preparation.

— Ten years of intense prayer that taught me what it meant to be "eating the carpet."
— Ten years of locking myself in with God on Friday and Saturday nights when most young men my age were out chasing girls and drinking themselves into oblivion.
— Ten years of putting off marriage or raising a family.
— Ten years of absorbing Scripture like a sponge; from Job to Malachi, from Abraham to the Apostles.

Digging for More

That was only the beginning. For the next ten years something entirely different happened. In a variety of ways, God began to drop deposits of precious gold into my mind, my heart and my spirit. Each revelation I received was separate and distinct, yet they fit together like the elements of an exquisite piece of jewelry.

Some days it seemed that a beam of heavenly light would flood God's message of abundance into my soul. At other times I felt like Jacob, and I had to climb high on the mountain to pitch my tent. I would wrestle with the Lord until I could lay claim to just one nugget of truth.

I remember when God would give me just one tiny morsel of manna — as small as one line or even one word. Then for the next six months, eight months, and often even longer, I would have my spiritual shovel out, digging for more.

Many times it seemed that I looked in the same place a thousand times before the answer came.

Suddenly, as I was reading, the Holy Spirit would energize certain words and cause them to miraculously raise up from the page.

The truth would leap into my life.

Abundance was not placed on earth to become a man-centered craving or a fleshly desire. What we're discussing is not about the size of your mansion or the horsepower of your custom sports coupe. As you will learn, it is a message that is at the very core of the kingdom of God. You need to understand it, operate in it and adopt it as your lifestyle.

As I look back on my journey, I realize that the Lord gave me each of these ten keys approximately one year apart. I believe it happened in that fashion so that I would not only be able to receive what God had for me, but I would be able to absorb and polish each nugget of truth before presenting it to you.

I vividly recall the times I would be studying at my desk and become so overwhelmed at what the Lord had revealed that I would literally jump to my feet.

> *I'd walk around my office*
> *and applaud God — shouting and*
> *praising the Lord for what*
> *He was showing me.*

Are you ready for twenty years of preparation and revelation to be yours in the time it takes you to read this book? Are you ready for God to do a quick work in you?

There's only one way for this great truth to come alive in your life. First, you must be *ready* to receive. Before you read another page, take a few minutes to examine your heart.

Ask yourself these vital questions:

- Have I fully repented of all my sin?
- Is Christ truly the Lord of my life?
- Am I ready to accept and act upon God's Word?
- Am I willing to invest the time and effort necessary to receive what God has in store for me?

- Will I acknowledge the source of my supply?
- Will I be reliable and trustworthy with the abundance the Lord will place in my hands?

If your answer is "Yes" to every question, get ready for an outpouring of God's blessing. I believe the skies will open and you'll be drenched from head to toe.

However, there may first be areas of your life that desperately need attention. I don't have to tell you what they are; you know exactly what I am talking about. Don't procrastinate. Get alone with the Lord until these issues are settled.

I can tell you from experience that *great revelation doesn't come without great preparation.* You can read this book a thousand times, until you are able to quote it from memory, but the words will have little effect until your heart is prepared to receive them. Otherwise, it will be like trying to plant an acorn in concrete. There will never be a majestic oak tree.

Taking Dominion

In a world steeped in mental, moral, spiritual and economic poverty, the concept of abundance is still foreign. The vast majority of people on our planet feel trapped in a web of hopelessness and defeat.

That's not how God planned it. When the Almighty created this beautiful, bountiful world, He also decreed that man should "have dominion" over it (Genesis 1:28). Not just part of the earth, but *all* of it.

In the annals of history, there are examples of men and women who have attempted to conquer certain domains, unique realms and specific kingdoms. Christopher Columbus discovered the New World. Sir Edmund Hillary was the first to climb Mount Everest. Dr. Jonas Salk found the vaccine that defeated the scourge of polio.

There have only been a few men, however, who have attempted to conquer the entire world. Alexander the Great was one of them.

He started early. When Alexander was only thirteen years of age he was a student of Aristotle, the noted Greek philosopher. Before long his father placed the entire kingdom of Macedonia in the hands of his son.

In 339 B.C., at the age of seventeen, he was found weeping on the portico steps of the palace. People gathered around him and asked, "Alexander, why do you weep?"

He looked at them and replied, "I weep because there are no more worlds to conquer." His marching armies had crushed the Persians, the Syrians and the Egyptians, yet he hungered for more.

More Than Enough

I believe there are dominions God has for us that we haven't even begun to subdue or master.

The apostle Paul asked the Christians at Rome what it would take to separate us from the Lord's blessing — "tribulation, or distress, or persecution, or famine, or nakedness, or peril, or sword?"

I get excited every time I read his answer. "No," he declared, "we are more than conquerors through him that loved us" (Romans 8:37).

That's right! We are *more* than an Edmund Hillary or an Alexander the Great. We are part of the victorious army of the King of Kings.

To everyone who will listen I say:

Stand tall and allow the Spirit of God to rise within you like a mighty giant!

It's time to break the syndrome of scarcity and want — the "missionary barrel" mentality that is always looking for hand-me-downs. Don't listen to what the sociologists, the welfare wardens or the media pessimists are predicting about your future. You have the authority to proclaim: "God has declared that I will live

13

in abundance and I will be *more* than a conqueror."

The keys you will soon hold in your hand will give you access to the spiritual storehouse of Jehovah Jireh, the name which means "God will provide."

Several years ago when the Lord drew back the curtains and began to give me a glimpse of just a portion of what He has now revealed, I couldn't wait to share it with my congregation. Compared to our present facility, the building was small. It had grown from 180 seats to over 1200, and more than 2500 were packed into the multiple services we held on Sunday mornings.

For several weeks I delivered my soul on the message God was giving me. Then one day a well-meaning gentleman in our church cornered some of our staff members and said, "You know, the pastor needs to stop preaching this. I love this church, but I'm telling you he's getting us in trouble."

He continued, "I'm not a person that is prone to visions, but every Sunday or Monday night I am tormented." The man exclaimed,

I have a dream that a gigantic monster is being created and it's coming through the ceiling and walking up and down and down the aisles of our church. It's going to devour the people.

The man was convinced that my messages on abundance were creating this Godzilla-like "monster." He wanted me to stop preaching on the topic.

One of our well-seasoned staff ministers wisely told him, "Well sir, I'll tell you what to do. Go and pray about it and ask God for the interpretation of the vision you are having. Have you done that yet?"

"Oh, no," the man responded.

The next week the man returned and announced, "We need to ask the pastor to preach more on this subject. Can't we add a seminar or a special class on this theme?"

The surprised staff minister said, "Wait a minute. Last week you wanted the pastor to stop because you thought a monster was being created. Now you want even *more* revelation on the topic. What caused such a change?"

"Well, you told me to pray about it, and I did," the man replied. "And God showed me that the monster is not being *created* by Pastor's preaching, he's being *unveiled* and *exposed*." Then he added, "He's been stealing our children and eating our finances. But now I know that this revelation is so we can unmask this monster of poverty. We need to get him out of our lives and allow the abundance of the Lord to be released!"

Setting Limits

I remember a recent discussion I had with a group of friends at a coffee shop.

I asked one fellow how he would respond if I said, "I think we should set a limit on how many individuals we allow to give their hearts to Christ. After all, isn't heaven going to be overcrowded? How many people do we snatch out of the corridors of the doomed before we say, 'Enough is enough!'"?

"Wait just a minute," one man protested. "We can't set limits on salvation."

To another I asked what he would think if I declared, "I believe it's time that God stops providing healing for you. Just think of all the times the Lord has touched your body. Shouldn't someone else be receiving miracles?"

He smiled and responded, "Look, I don't mind God healing someone else, but I don't want Him to stop restoring me."

When we began discussing abundance, however, the reaction was totally different. The topic made them nervous, and some wanted to limit God. "Oh, if I had money," one man commented, "I might buy a boat and use it on Sunday instead of going to church."

"In that case," I responded, "you don't need abundance, you need salvation." I told them that is like saying, "Well, if God healed my body I might leave the kingdom and play tennis every weekend because I feel so good."

> *It is not up to you and me*
> *to decide how much is too much.*
> *That's God's business, not ours.*

It may come as a shock to you, but the Lord has volumes to say about our success — both spiritually and materially. The problem is that the teaching has been largely ignored by the leading voices of the church.

Revelations are somewhat dispensational. They have been released for specific needs at certain times. For example, Martin Luther's great Reformation was based on a simple truth: *The just shall live by faith.* That's the message the world of his day so desperately needed.

In the late 1940s, 1950s, and into the early 1960s there was a worldwide healing revival of enormous proportions. It was as if the Lord was saying, "I am still your healer."

Physical restoration didn't stop with the healing of blind Bartimaeus or the woman with the issue of blood. The Lord was telling us, "I *was* your healer, I *am* your healer, and I *will be* your healer."

What is the Lord's great revelation for today's

generation? It is a truth that has been abused, ridiculed, misunderstood and often ignored — Our God is a God of abundance.

A Prophetic Voice

There's a wonderful verse in the Book of Proverbs I have quoted countless times: "Where there is no vision, the people perish" (Proverbs 29:18).

What kind of vision was the writer talking about? It was more than foresight; it was a voice. The Scripture can be paraphrased as, "Where there is no prophetic unction or voice, the people perish."

Vision is not the imagination of man, but what God imparts to His people. Without it the people "perish" — or, they cast off all restraint and run wild.

That's also an accurate picture of ninety percent of the church world. They have disregarded divine mandates and are marching to their own drum beat, without direction.

Have you ever seen a river without banks? I certainly haven't. Without banks, it would become a swamp.

A vision can take a stinky, stagnant swamp and begin to squeeze it and raise the banks until there are boundaries and protection. The water begins to flow and suddenly there is life. Even greater, the waters can be harnessed to produce enormous power.

That's what a vision can do.

Your True Father

Just as a river flows on a steady course, God, your Father, has a well-designed plan for you.

Paul said something quite unusual to the Christians at Corinth. He stated, "Though ye have ten thousand instructors in Christ, yet have ye not many fathers" (1 Corinthians 4:15). Then the apostle added, "I have begotten you through the gospel."

It's still true today. You find people everywhere spouting their own version of the Gospel — saint and sinner alike. Sadly, it's not a prophetic vision or anointed revelation.

Paul was saying, "Here's how you will recognize a true father. He begets you in the Lord."

A loving dad will pay whatever sacrifice is necessary to see you are birthed into and advanced in the kingdom of God.

> *As we are painfully aware,*
> *a father is not a father just*
> *because he can produce a child. No.*
> *He must provide and protect.*

What happens if a father fails to take responsibility? "But if any provide not for his own, and specially for those of his own house, he hath denied the faith and is

19

worse than an infidel" (1 Timothy 5:8).

Paul is not only talking about a natural father, but of the household of faith. It's a prophetic revelation of who Jesus Christ is in our lives.

God says, "I am your father and am responsible for you. I have a plan for you."

Subtle Strategies

Satan also has a plan. The attack that hit your life today from the kingdom of darkness wasn't devised a few minutes ago. It is likely the devil has been strategically working on it for months, years — and possibly for generations. He cleverly arranged to maneuver you into a position of weakness. Then he launched his assault.

The techniques he uses are subtle — a suggestive smile from a co-worker; the urge to embellish your past on a job application; the temptation to take funds when no one is watching.

How can we safeguard ourselves against Satan's cunning devices? The Word tells us to "Put on the whole armour of God, that ye may be able to stand against the wiles (strategies) of the devil" (Ephesians 6:11).

Now for the good news! *Just as the devil has a plan to take you out, God has a plan to keep you in!*

The Lord I serve was present long before the serpent arrived and will be here when that ugly creature is gone. You see, God knows *everything*. He knew the seed that would make the tree that would be formed into the chair on which you are sitting. The Almighty had you in mind when the seed fell to the ground.

God also has a strategy for your resources that is greater than any advice you'll ever receive from the most prominent financial planner.

Since vision is foreknowledge, you need to know that God has been working on your situation before you were ever born. My Bible declares, "Forget not the Lord your God, for it is he that giveth thee the power to get wealth, that he may establish his covenant in the earth" (Deuteronomy 8:18).

I believe that World Harvest Church was already here before James Parsley ever met Ellen Parsley and had a son named Rod. In God's eyes it was a reality, but He had to work His plan.

There's something else we need to know. God has taken the responsibility to thwart the "seed eater" on your behalf. He declares, "And I will rebuke the devourer for your sakes" (Malachi. 3:11).

I can tell you on the authority of heaven that the Lord will chart the course for His abundance to be released into your life. This process is vital because you can then release that same abundance into His kingdom and help bring back His Son. That is why I say:

God wants you in abundance more than you want to be there!

There came a point in my life when I stopped being governed by what I saw, what I read, or what I heard. Instead, I became faithful to the heavenly vision — God's revelation. As Paul stated, "I have received of the Lord that which also I delivered unto you" (1 Corinthians 11:23).

What I am sharing is not something I dreamed. God *birthed this* message deep within me by His sovereign will.

Before the Beginning

If you think that the Creator casually tossed a world into space and has been making up the rules as He goes along, you and I are not reading the same Bible.

Pay close attention to this: "For whom he did foreknow, he also did predestinate to be conformed to the image of his Son, that he might be the firstborn among many brethren" (Romans 8:29).

How extensive is God's foreknowledge? It began at the very foundation of the world. "And all that dwell upon the earth shall worship him, whose names are not written in the book of life of the Lamb slain from the foundation of the world" (Revelation 13:8).

What do I say to a person who doesn't believe the Lord has a specific design for them? Before He set the world on its framework; before He ever declared "Light be" and light *was;* before Adam ever took a breath or Eve ever walked a step, God had a master plan.

Long before the world was spoken into being, something happened in the heart and mind of God. Outside of Jerusalem on a lonely hill, He slayed His Son. Why? Because it was His responsibility to protect and provide for you. He is your Father.

Think of it! Before you were ever in existence God lavished His love on you! He caused the heavens to go black, and He smote His Son because He knew the day would come when you would bow your knee and say, "Lord, I need help. I can't make it by myself."

Then you hear His voice saying, "It's okay. I've taken care of it. Provision has already been made."

What a God! It makes me want to sing, "When I think of His goodness, and all He's done for me, I could shout, run, and dance all night!"

I get goose bumps when I realize that we serve a God who supplies *before* there is a need. You don't have to wait for a blessing. He has *already* anointed your head with oil.

Here's something I want you to think about for the rest of your life:

If you have a need, that's proof that the supply has already been given! It's already there.

Regardless of the economic situation you may be in at this very moment, remember, God has already provided.

To the worried mother who says, "My son needs a new pair of glasses," or the concerned father who wonders, "How am I going to meet the mortgage payment this month?" God knows your need before you ever ask, and He wants you to recognize Him as your source.

Not only will the Lord provide, He'll protect you by stopping Satan dead in His tracks. He tells the enemy, "You can't get to them without first coming through me."

God spoke through the prophet Jeremiah and declared that He intends for you to prosper and not to fail. "For I know the thoughts that I think toward you, saith the Lord, thoughts of peace, and not of evil" (Jeremiah 29:11).

For years I've known people who constantly try to tell the Lord what His plan is. They say, "Well, I need to stay poor. It keeps me humble."

Don't make the foolish attempt to outguess God. You'll never do it. His objective is to prosper you in blessing, in power, in righteousness, in authority and in abundance.

Closer Than You Think

In his famous book, *Acres of Diamonds*, Russell Conwell tells the fascinating story of a man who traveled the world in a futile search for diamonds. When he returned, he discovered them in his own backyard — acres of them.

Where do we find God's answer? Where can we go to uncover His plan? He has hidden His secret with you! "For the froward (the perverse) is abomination to the Lord, but his secret is with the righteous" (Proverbs 3:32).

The first time I saw those words I read them again and again. I thought, "Does that mean that I know something I don't know? Do I understand something I don't understand?" Absolutely.

The answer is inside you and has been there since the day you were born. If you'll start excavating and searching, you'll find it.

What we already possess is more valuable than the secret ingredients in Coca-Cola™ or Kentucky Fried Chicken™.

When you discover God's secret, the world will offer any price to take it from you. Yet they can never know what you possess because the secret is not for the unrighteous, but for those who are pure before the Lord. The prophet Amos declared, the Lord "revealeth his secret unto his servants the prophets" (Amos 3:7).

Facing the Facts

Why is this revelation so vital? Consider these statistics:

- At retirement, ninety percent of American families families cannot write a check for $5,000 even though they earned in excess of $1 million during their working years.
- Today, eighty percent of U.S. families owe more than they own.
- Nine out of ten families live paycheck to paycheck.

- The present average level of giving in America's church families varies betweeen 2.3 and 3.8 percent of their income.
- Only eighteen percent of church-attending evangelical Christians biblically tithe.

After learning these facts, it didn't take me long to realize that the church is attempting to fulfill the Great Commission on only twenty percent of its potential power and efficiency. What if that could be raised to sixty, seventy, or even eighty percent. We would evangelize the nations at such an astounding pace that millions would be swept into the kingdom.

The world may be sinking in a cesspool of debt, yet I am convinced the problem is not a shortage of money, but a shortage of morality. It's not a lack of resources, but a lack of righteousness. We need to recognize that God has established some specific principles He expects us to follow. They are a vital, essential part of His plan for you.

Make it Plain

When my twenty-year odyssey with the revelation of God's abundance concluded I asked the Lord, "What happens now? What do you expect me to do with this truth?"

As clear as any voice I have ever heard, God spoke

27

to me and said,

Don't wait. Proclaim it to all who will listen. Write the message I have given.

I felt like Habakkuk who declared, "I will stand upon my watch, and set me upon the tower, and will watch to see what he will say unto me, and what I shall answer when I am reproved. And the Lord answered me, and said, Write the vision, and make it plain upon the tables, that he may run that readeth it" (Habakkuk 2:1,2).

In the prophetic word written on these pages you will discover provision and protection, supply and security. God has promised that if you will follow His blueprint for your future — even if you don't completely understand it — you'll be released into its blessing.

Just as God gave them to me, here are the ten golden keys to your abundance.

GOLDEN KEY #1

THE PROCESS
OF EXCHANGE

"How fast are we going?" I asked the driver who was taking me on a forty mile run to the airport. "It seems like we're crawling."

"Oh, we're doing about 60 miles an hour," he replied.

Cars were whizzing by like lightning. "What's the speed limit on this road?" I asked curiously.

He pointed to a little sign on the side of the German highway that read: "Autobahn."

"On this road you can drive as fast as you please," he explained. "Even if they posted a speed limit everyone would just ignore it."

Amazed, I continued, "Do you mean to tell me you can push that pedal to the floor and you won't see a flashing light? You won't get a ticket?"

"That's right," he told me as we cruised along in his BMW 735I.

I smiled and suggested, "Why don't we see what this little puppy will do?"

"You asked for it," he said as my head snapped back and we almost doubled our speed. It was the ride of my life.

I thought, "What good is driving 60 miles an hour on the autobahn? I'm in a new kingdom. The rules have changed."

Two Vital Words

Several years ago, when God gave me the first key to His revelation of abundance, I was reading in the book of Deuteronomy when two simple words riveted my attention.

The words were these: "Come in."

"What could they possibly mean?" I wondered.

Here is the verse I was reading. "And it shall be, when thou art come in unto the land which the Lord thy God giveth thee for an inheritance, and possessest it, and dwellest therein; that thou shalt take of the first of all the fruit of the earth, which thou shalt bring of thy land that the Lord thy God giveth thee, and shalt put it in a basket. and shalt go unto the place which the Lord thy God shall choose to place his name there" (Deuteronomy 26:1,2).

KEY #1: THE PROCESS OF EXCHANGE

I prayed, "Lord, what is this new land you are talking about, and what does it mean that I am to "come in?"

The Lord responded, "Trust me. I'm going to exchange what you have for something far greater."

At that moment the Lord had given me Golden Key #1: *The process of exchange.*

My friend, everything about your life is involved in a trade-off.

- You exhale so you may be able to inhale.
- You put your clothes on to take them off, and put them on again.
- You walk into a room only to leave it. You leave the room only to return again.
- You sit down so you may stand up. You stand up so you may sit down.

Have you ever been in a crowded room with no ventilation? The air not only becomes stuffy and stagnant, but the oxygen is rapidly used up. Before long you are literally struggling to breathe.

What would happen if you chose not to replace the liquids in your body? You would become dehydrated and would eventually die.

I'm sure you've listened to the story of someone

31

who has been delivered from alcohol or drugs. The process is two-fold. They not only tell you what they were rescued *from*. They rejoice at what they were delivered *to*.

Consider your mail. Just because you put a stamp on an envelope and drop it in a post box doesn't mean it's been delivered. That only happens when it arrives at its destination.

Here's how God's process of exchange works. He brings you out of the kingdom of the world and into His glorious kingdom. Why? So that you may then go back into the kingdom of the world and bring others into His kingdom.

This same basic principle applies to your finances.

Before you can receive what is in God's hand, you first have to unclench your fist and offer the Lord what is in your hand.

I've met some people who are so bound by what they own, they refuse to let go. As a result, they don't experience God's abundance.

You will never enter God's kingdom by leaving one foot in the world. You can't straddle the fence. Paul told the believers at Corinth, "Wherefore come out from among them, and be ye separate, saith the Lord, and touch not the unclean thing; and I will receive you, and will be a Father unto you, and ye shall be my sons and daughters, saith the Lord Almighty" (2 Corinthians 6:17,18).

There are some individuals who have to be pulled from the world kicking and screaming. They can't stand the thought of giving up their personal possessions and material resources. The problem isn't new.

On the way to the Promised Land, the last thing to leave the kingdom of darkness and the land of bondage was the cattle. Those herds represented wealth, and that was the last bastion of satanic resistance before the children of Israel experienced total freedom.

Don't forget, however, the Israelites who came into the promised land were the same ones who had come out of captivity. Scripture declares, He has "delivered us from the power of darkness, and hath translated us into the kingdom of his dear Son" (Colossians 1:13).

Coming Out

How do you come out of the world and into God's kingdom? There are three important things that take place.

1. You come out positionally.

Your spirit is changed. The moment you are born again, your heavenly Father actually adopts you and restores you to the relationship with Him for which you were originally intended.

Since your true home is no longer on earth but in God's kingdom, your position is changed. You have said "Goodbye" to darkness and are walking in sunshine.

2. You come out experientially.

Your soul is changed. We know that the Lord transforms us, but we have some obligations too. Righteousness is what God does. Holiness is what we do. He deals with our character, we deal with our conduct.

The areas of our soul, including our mind, our will and our emotions are domains He expects us to subdue.

3. You come out ultimately.

Ultimate sanctification is sometimes called glorification. This process takes place in our new dwelling place in heaven. It is when every need — financial, spiritual, etc., is ultimately met.

Jesus said that we should pray for His will to be done "in earth, as it is in heaven" (Matthew 6:10). Heaven's resources dwell in earthen vessels, and what is in heaven now, and prepared for us in the future, can be part of our daily life. As born again believers, it is our birthright to experience heaven's blessings on earth.

Jesus declared, "The kingdom of God is within you" (Luke 17:21).

What we're discussing makes absolutely no sense to a Wall Street broker because the stock exchange doesn't understand God's system of accounting. Try telling this to your banker: "I'm going to give what I have so I can possess what I don't have."

Brand New Rules

Everything in the new Kingdom is diametrically opposed to that of the old. In heaven's economy:

- To go up, we must first go down. The Lord exalts the man who humbles himself.
- To live we must first die — to self, to desires, and to the flesh.
- To receive, we must first give — it's the law of sowing and reaping.
- To bring us out, God brings us in — out of the shadows and into His glorious light.

With our narrow, finite mind, it is so easy to become a pessimist. We look around and moan, "Well, I can only make this much money, save this much and invest this much at this percentage rate."

When you understand God's process of exchange it's totally different. What kind of return does He promise? When our seed is sown in good ground we can expect a yield of "thirtyfold, some sixty, and some a hundred" (Mark 4:20). And He was not talking about some future time. It can happen *now!*

How is that possible? Because we're living in a new kingdom.

There is no limit on God's abundance. It's like dining at a sumptuous smorgasbord and filling your plate again and again.

You can expect even more at the Lord's table. "But the fruit of the Spirit is love, joy, peace, longsuffering, gentleness, goodness, faith, meekness, temperance: against such there is no law" (Galatians 5:22,23).

What do those last two words say? "No law!"

The restrictions have been removed. There are no limits — nothing to hold you back. You can have as much joy as you want and all the faith you need.

People like to talk about a new world order, but I'll take the one God established in His Word. When you move into His divine realm, you can have unlimited abundance. You are no longer bound by the world's restrictions.

KEY #1: THE PROCESS OF EXCHANGE

"No limit living" is marvelous, but it's not a one way street. If the Lord is willing to give everything He has, He expects us to do the same.

I remember hearing a minister complain, "Well, if I did everything God told me to do I'd be worn out!" Perhaps that's why the man's church was struggling for survival.

To be perfectly honest, I could get tired just *thinking* about my schedule. A typical week for me is preaching at World Harvest Church on Sunday morning, Sunday night and Wednesday, producing daily and weekly television programs, running a preschool-12 Christian academy, a Bible college and supervising several hundred employees.

What do you do when, on top of everything else, the Lord says, "And by the way, I want you to spend 150 nights a year on the road"?

One night, totally drained, I said, "Lord, I'm not sure I can continue."

He asked, "Did I tell you to do it?"

"Yes," I replied.

"Then whose plan is it?" He wanted to know

"It's yours, Lord."

That's when I realized that I have to give Him every ounce of energy I have — without limits.

You see, when I traded in my old life for a new one, I was totally transformed.

■ I'm not the person I used to be.

- I don't live where I used to live.
- I don't think as I used to think.
- I don't go where I used to go.

No longer am I in the kingdom of this world. I've been promoted and transferred to a higher place. And I won't say "No" to my King.

A Bowl of Soup

There's a great price to pay when we make the wrong exchange. It's a lesson we can learn from Esau, the firstborn son of Isaac and Rebecca.

He and his twin brother, Jacob, were opposites. Esau was a skillful hunter who loved to roam the open country. Jacob was a "mamma's boy" who stayed in the family tent and learned how to turn the pea-like lentils that grew in bad soil into some pretty good reddish-brown stew.

One day, after a long, unsuccessful hunting expedition, Esau came home, weary to the point of exhaustion.

Jacob said, "Don't worry. You're home now. What would you like to eat?"

"Quick. Give me some of that stew," he demanded of his brother. "I'm famished."

Jacob, knowing how hungry his brother was, offered to feed him on one condition. He said, "Sell me this day thy birthright" (Genesis 25:31).

Esau thought, "Well, I am about to die. What good is this document to me? I certainly can't eat it!"

He pulled the piece of paper out of his pocket and agreed to the exchange. He traded his birthright for a bowl of pottage.

Many years later, when Jacob was an old man, there was a great famine in the land. He sent his sons on a lengthy journey into Egypt, hoping they would find provisions.

Still protecting his birthright, he said, "My sons, I am praying that you will find something for us to eat."

Jacob's grandfather, Abraham, was given a covenant blessing by God. Speaking about Abraham's descendants, God declared:

I will bless them that bless thee, and curse him that curseth thee; and in thee shall all families of the earth be blessed (Genesis 12:3).

Months later, Jacob looked out on the horizon and saw a little puff of dust. He squinted his eyes and rejoiced, "Yes, it is my sons!"

But he didn't hear the clanging of empty wagons. When they returned they were "laden with the good things of Egypt" (Genesis 45:23).

I see people everywhere who are the mirror image

of Esau. They are ruled by their cravings and emotions. They sell their souls for a bowl of soup and are destined for lives of continual hunger.

The writer of Hebrews said about Esau: "For ye know how that afterward, when he would have inherited the blessing, he was rejected: for he found no place of repentance, though he sought it carefully with tears" (Hebrews 12:17).

Think twice before you make the wrong choice. Jesus proclaimed, "For what is a man profited, if he shall gain the whole world, and lose his own soul? or what shall a man give in exchange for his soul?" (Matthew 16:26).

The covenant blessing is our birthright as born again children of God. Never let it go. It holds the promise of God's continual supply.

Here and Now

What was the major theme of Christ when He walked on earth? It was the message of the kingdom of God. "Jesus went about all Galilee, teaching in their synagogues, and preaching the gospel of the kingdom" (Matthew 4:23).

When people hear the word "kingdom" they immediately think about heaven. But that's not what the Lord was talking about. The kingdom is now. And it is here — on earth. Christ said, "Repent, for the kingdom of heaven is at hand" (Matthew 4:17).

The kingdom comes when the King arrives. And Jesus came to earth 2000 years ago to establish a heavenly order on earth.

The Lord taught His disciples to pray by using these words: "Thy kingdom come. Thy will be done in earth, as it is in heaven" (Matthew 6:10).

As a born again believer you are *in* the world but not *of* the world. That's why it is vital that we never allow the culture of iniquity to seep into the dominion Christ came to establish.

> *God's kingdom is a theocracy, not a democracy. It's not up for a vote. Christ is our King and we are His loyal subjects.*

Every time we bow before His throne we acknowledge His royal Kingship.

As a child of God, what I possess is not mine. I'm only the trustee — the custodian. It belongs to the treasury of my King.

Recently I spoke to a farmer who had part of his land taken by the government for the extension of a new road. "There was nothing I could do about it," he lamented. They said they had eminent domain."

Many people don't realize that the federal authorities have the right to seize whatever they want — regardless of who paid for it.

That is also the way God operates, but He has always had that right.

When Jesus was ready to make His triumphal entry into Jerusalem He didn't say, "Go out and buy me a donkey." No. He told two of His disciples to go into the nearby village, and they would find a donkey tied and a small colt with her. "Loose them and bring them unto me," Christ commanded. "And if any man say ought unto you, ye shall say, 'The Lord hath need of them'" (Matthew 21:2,3).

Why did the Lord make such a demand? Two reasons. First, it was to fulfill a prophecy of Zechariah (Zechariah 9:9). And second, everything belongs to Him. "The earth is the Lord's, and the fullness thereof" (Psalm 24:1).

A Total Turn-Around

The process of exchange begins with repentance. That's the only passport that will be recognized at the gates of God's kingdom.

What does it mean to repent? It is when our soul is changed toward God and we are headed in a totally new direction.

The apostle Paul tells us how that happens: "I

42

beseech you therefore, brethren, by the mercies of God, that ye present your bodies a living sacrifice, holy, acceptable unto God, which is your reasonable service. And be not conformed to this world: but be ye transformed by the renewing of your mind that ye may prove what is that good and acceptable, and perfect will of God" (Romans 12:1,2).

The transformation includes a mind that is renewed and a heart that is cleansed by the blood of Christ.

Abundance is the work of the soul. That's what John stated when he revealed what was "Number one" on his prayer list. He prayed:

Beloved, I wish above all things that thou mayest prosper and be in health, even as thy soul prospereth (3 John 2).

Your soul has three distinct areas: your mind, your will, and your emotions. Here is how they must be transformed in order to experience God's abundance.

1. Your mind must be changed.

God's Word will give you a new view of your resources. You are not a child of less, you're a child of more. You're not a child of poverty, but a child of provision. "Let this mind be in you, which was also in

Christ Jesus" (Philippians 2:5).

2. Your will must be submitted.

Two of the greatest barriers to blessing are stubbornness and conceit. Those who believe they have all the answers don't leave much room for God.

It's not the Lord's intention to *break* your will. His only desire is that you surrender yourself to Him. "Submit yourselves therefore to God" (James 4:7).

3. Your emotions must be controlled.

When self-discipline is combined with God's abundance, the results can be phenomenal. For example, you can't always have everything you want when you want it. Just because you have a credit card doesn't mean you have to charge it to the limit.

Somewhere along the line we have to break the cycle of debt. Can you imagine what would happen if you not only gave God His tithe, but invested an additional ten percent of your earnings in your future?

Is it a Sin?

A dear lady once asked me, "Pastor, why do you talk so much about money?""

My response was, "Why shouldn't I? After all, one out of every six verses in the four Gospels refers to finances."

Money is simply a medium of exchange, nothing more, nothing less. It is how we use our resources that makes the difference. For example, it's not money, but the "love of money" that is the "root of all evil" (1 Timothy 6:10).

Sin is not the absence of law but the failure to obey God's requirements and standards.

Is sex a sin? Not if it remains inside the covenant of marriage. But outside the law it becomes a tragic transgression. When we seek to fulfill a desire, even a Godly desire, in a way not prescribed in the law, we are guilty of iniquity.

Tossed by the Wind

To successfully exchange your old world for God's kingdom, your focus needs to be totally unclouded. As James wrote, "But let him ask in faith, nothing wavering. For he that wavereth is like a wave of the sea driven with the wind and tossed. For let not that man think that he shall receive any thing of the Lord. A double minded man is unstable in all his ways." (James 1:6-8).

Have you ever been around someone who vacillates — who can't make up his mind? Today he says, "Yes, I believe God is a God of abundance. Tomorrow he hesitates, saying, "I'm not sure." That's not being double minded, it's being confused.

45

The double-minded man is in a struggle between his soul and his spirit, between his heart and his mind.

When a missionary presents the need for a massive Bible distribution program in Asia, a tug of war begins inside of you. Your spirit — that always agrees with the Word — says, "Write out that $500 check." But your soul, with its mind, its will, and its emotions, whispers, "Don't you really need some new clothes?"

Your spirit says, "I'm the head and not the tail," while your soul is saying the complete opposite.

Would you like to know the secret of having this problem removed from your life forever?

Here it is: *Accept God's line of authority to totally govern your life.* Scripture declares that God has "put all things under his (Christ's) feet, and gave him to be the head over all things to the church" (Ephesians 1:22).

In God's kingdom, you are not the final decision maker. That right belongs to the King. How do I know? "In the beginning was the Word, and the Word was with God, and the Word was God" (John 1:1) "And the Word was made flesh and dwelt among us" (v.14).

If you will submit your financial future to the headship of Christ, you'll experience the freedom and security His authority brings. Finally, you will be able to say a permanent "Farewell" to both confusion and double mindedness. You'll come out of the land of bondage and see the sign: "Welcome to liberty and abundance."

When you begin to use this golden key, you can expect some great things to transpire.

- **Your income will be changed.** "The wealth of the sinner is laid up for the just" (Proverbs 13:22).
- **Your investments will be changed.** "Lend, hoping for nothing again, and your reward shall be great" (Luke 6:35).
- **Your giving will be changed.** "Give, and it shall be given unto you; good measure, pressed down, and shaken together, and running over" (Luke 6:38).
- **Your life will be changed.** "Therefore if any man be in Christ, he is a new creature: old things are passed away; behold, all things are become new" (2 Corinthians 5:17).

That is the greatest exchange of all!

GOLDEN KEY #2

THE PROCESS OF POSSESSION
(GOING TO WAR)

It was a bitter winter day in Columbus, Ohio, when the Lord clearly spoke to me. "I want you to go next door and possess the land," He directed.

I was in my office at the former location of our church. Dressed in a business suit, I left my desk and walked into that corn field.

Obeying God, I walked around the field and said, "In the name of Jesus Christ of Nazareth, every place the sole of my foot touches, I am going to receive an inheritance from the Lord."

The crop had been cut after the harvest, and the short, frozen corn stalks were jabbing into my legs and digging into the pants of the suit I was wearing. I kept walking. "Devil," I said, "It makes no difference who owns this land right now. I'm telling you that I declare war in the realm of the Spirit. I'm going to take it! I'm going to plant the flag of the kingdom of God on this property. We are going to possess this land in the name of the Lord."

It happened.

God told the children of Israel: And it shall be, when thou art come in unto the land which the Lord thy God giveth thee for an inheritance, and possessest it, and dwellest therein" (Deuteronomy 26:1).

Golden Key #2 involves *the process of possession.* God's abundance is there for the taking, but you have to possess your spiritual territory.

Taking the Spoils

Ask any army strategist and you'll learn that "possession" is a military term that indicates you have invaded, occupied and taken the spoils of the previous tenants.

Right now, we are in a major battle against the enemy of our souls. This is not the millennium. The lions aren't laying down with the lambs.

We are taking back what is ours. We're not saying, "I wonder what he thinks about it." We have taken charge and we're driving Satan out.

This is the time for "spoiling." Someone has stolen what belongs to you, and God is commanding, "It's yours! Go get it!"

When you win a battle, the bounty is yours. The Lord does not keep it from you. As the psalmist declared, "No good thing will he withhold from them that walk uprightly" (Psalm 84:11).

You may say, "Well, I thought that as a Christian what I receive would just happen — abundance would be automatic."

Nothing happens by accident. God does His part and He expects us to do ours.

I once heard about a man who lived near a dilapidated house that was literally falling apart. Every time he drove past the eye-sore he wanted to look the other way. The shingles had fallen from the roof, the paint was cracked and peeling and the weeds were knee high.

Then one day, to his surprise, he noticed major changes. The lawn was mowed. The shutters were straight. The gate had been fixed and there was a fresh coat of paint.

The neighbor walked up to the house and met the tenant who had just moved in. "You and the Lord have done a good job with this place," he commented.

The new owner, with sweat dripping from his brow and a broom in his hand, smiled and said, "You should have seen it when the Lord had it on His own!"

The building that houses World Harvest Church didn't just "happen." God didn't say, "I think I'll place an enormous sanctuary on that lot." No, the structure was constructed board by board, nail by nail, with a great amount of blood, sweat, and tears. We physically possessed the land.

I love the story of Joshua and Caleb, two of the twelve men who were sent by Moses to spy out the land of Canaan. Ten of the spies returned with a frightening report. With fear in their eyes, they exclaimed, "And there we saw the giants . . . and we were in our own sight as grasshoppers" (Numbers 13:33).

Joshua and Caleb did not see it that way. Yes, there were giants in the land, but they declared, "Let us go up at once, and possess it; for we are well able to overcome it" (v.30).

God didn't drive out the Amalekites, the Hittites, the Jebusites, and the rest of the "ites." It was Joshua, Caleb and the other children of Israel who were inspired by the Lord to chase the giants from the land. God promised that the territory would be theirs, but they had to possess it.

Our thinking needs to be transformed. We are not grasshoppers but giant-killers.

It's time for a declaration of war. Stand up and proclaim: "I'm drawing a line in the spiritual sand."

Not only are you commanding Satan to stay where he is, but you're saying, "I'm invading your territory, devil. "I'm going to take back what is rightfully mine!"

The evil one has walked into your home and has stolen your treasure. It doesn't belong to him — and never has. You don't need to feel guilty about launching your attack to retrieve the bounty. It was yours to begin with.

God was not going to physically fight the battles of the Israelites, but He promised to empower them to go forth and conquer. Following every skirmish, the Lord poured out His abundance. "Look," they said after a victory, "We have cattle to feed our families. We have equipment to dig our wells. We have tools to harvest the land."

Then, as they gave tithes and offerings back to God, He blessed them even more.

Battle Gear

You are at war! That's why you need to equip yourself for combat — from head to toe. The Word tells you to "Put on the whole armor of God, that ye may be able to stand against the wiles of the devil" (Ephesians 6:11).

The conflict is being fought on many fronts. "For

we wrestle not against flesh and blood, but against principalities, against powers, against the rulers of the darkness of this world, against spiritual wickedness in high places" (v.12).

Here is your battle gear.

- Have your loins "girt about with truth" (v.14).
- Put on "the breastplate of righteousness" (v.14).
- Your feet must be "shod with the preparation of the gospel of peace" (v.15).
- "Above all," put on "the shield of faith, wherewith ye shall be able to quench all the fiery darts of the wicked" (v.16).
- Protect your head with "the helmet of salvation" (v.17).
- In your hand hold "the sword of the Spirit, which is the word of God" (v.17).

Now you are prepared and ready. Draw your sword from its sheath and declare war against the kingdom of darkness.

How dare the devil tell us what we can and cannot do. We can defeat the enemy anywhere — on a corn field in Ohio or in a cocaine den in the Orient.

Dr. Lester Sumrall, my mentor in the ministry, went to Russia with a prophetic message from God. To people who had a poverty mentality, he said, "You're going to have to get your eyes off of your own problems. You must realize this is not someone else's mission field. This is *your* field. And you need to start to give."

It took boldness to preach that message in Moscow where it takes nearly one week's salary to buy four ounces of rancid meat. Dr. Sumrall told the people that God wanted them to defeat Satan in their own backyards. Then he took an offering to be used to rebuild a church in the north of Russia that the government had bulldozed.

A man recently told me, "I'm working in the inner city. It's impossible to prosper here. We have to depend on people's generosity."

"That's not true," I replied. "We all have something to contribute. God is not unfaithful. He gives everyone some kind of seed. Teach the people the miracle of giving."

On Alert

People refer to "the nation of Israel," but it is not as much a nation as it is an army. It's always been that way. The country doesn't have a traditional fighting force of volunteers. Instead, *everyone* is a member of the military.

The minute students graduate from high school — both young men and young women — they immediately start their training to be soldiers.

In the U.S. our reserve troops, the "weekend warriors" serve by choice. In Israel, every able-bodied adult in the nation is permanently on reserve, ready to be activated at a moment's notice.

This is our heritage. We are warriors with enemies to overcome.

We may not be embroiled in a conflict with the Canaanites, but we are fighting the battle of *greed*. "Not only do I want my ninety percent, but I want God's ten percent, too."

We may not be in an altercation with the Amorites, but we are battling *fear*. "I'm afraid that if I let go of what is in my hand toward God, He won't let go of what's in His hand toward me."

Fear stifles the church from fulfilling its destiny. It is why we do not witness and why we don't pray. Fear is behind ninety percent of our failures.

Here's a question I continue to ask:

What would you attempt for God if you knew it was impossible to fail?

56

When I hear the answer, I follow up with this question: "Well, what's stopping you?"

God gave a direct order when He declared, "Fear thou not" (Isaiah 41:10). It isn't an option.

He also tells you *why* you no longer need to worry. "For I am with thee: be not dismayed; for I am thy God: I will strengthen thee; yea, I will help thee: yea, I will uphold thee with the right hand of my righteousness" (v.10).

How do you counteract fear? With faith.

It's true that fear and faith cannot coexist in the same heart. They are mutually exclusive.

Abraham was strong in the faith, because he did not waiver or vacillate.

Why was the faith of the father of the nation of Israel so powerful? He did not slide back and forth between two opinions. It's a common fault among Christians. When they receive their paychecks on Friday afternoon their faith is sky-high. But by Saturday morning when they balance their accounts, fear has replaced their expectations.

Here is something I want to etch into your consciousness:

> *Where there is doubt concerning*
> *God's will to prosper you,*
> *perfect faith cannot exist.*

Why is this true? Because when the will of God is known, faith comes alive and fear dies.

Lack of information can destroy the seed you have sown. "By knowledge shall the chambers be filled with all precious and pleasant riches" (Proverbs 24:4). Just as the knowledge of God's will leads to abundance, ignorance leads to poverty.

The question is not, "Does God have unlimited resources to give me?" We need to ask, "Is it God's will to abundantly bless me financially?"

When you seek the Lord, you'll find the answer is "Yes." And when you *know* God's will, you can *trust* His will.

Abraham was not just rich. He was extremely wealthy. Yet he used his resources wisely.

God's abundance is not granted to lavish on yourself. It is given to establish the kingdom of God throughout the earth.

We are created to be vessels. For example, my blood vessels are not the producers of my blood, they are simply carriers of life forces. And that's what we are to be. You might even say we're "delivery boys."

God says, "Here is abundance. Loose it in the earth

and help bring my kingdom."

If the Lord had not wanted you to prosper He would not have created prosperity, because abundance is not a promise; it is a fact.

The Lord takes pleasure in the success of His servants. Long ago the psalmist declared, "I have been young, and now am old; yet have I not seen the righteous forsaken, nor his seed begging bread" (Psalm 37:25).

Don't Trust Your Feelings

Faith not only allows you to wage good warfare, but makes it possible to march into enemy territory and be victorious.

Fear is produced by False Evidence that only Appears to be Real. You may think it is logical and authentic, but it isn't. It is produced by our senses — by what we see, hear, touch, taste, and feel.

- Esau's nose cost him his birthright — he could smell that bowl of stew.
- Samson's heart cost him his strength — he weakened in the hands of Delilah.
- Peter's eyes cost him a walk on the water — he looked at the storm instead of the Savior.

When Jesus approached the grave of Lazarus, His sense of smell told him the man was dead. Scripture records, "By this time he stinketh: for he hath been dead four days" (John 11:39). His body was cold and clammy.

The Lord didn't see him through the eyes of man, but through the eyes of faith. He cried with a loud voice, "Lazarus, come forth" (v.43).

Never, never, never trust your feelings. Trust only God's Word.

Those who pilot small aircraft need to be not only visually rated (VFR), but instrument rated (IFR). The moment may come when you are in a storm or a "whiteout" and lose all sense of direction. They can be a victim of vertigo and not know if they're upside down or sideways. There's no reference point.

That's when they lock onto their instruments and give them their total trust and confidence.

The Word of God is your IFR — your instrument guidance system. Without it you could send your life into a bridge or a mountain.

Satan attacks our senses. The Holy Spirit, however, is guiding every area of our existence.

While fear is motivated by our feelings, faith is

"the substance of things hoped for, the evidence of things not seen" (Hebrews 11:1).

When I attended Bible college, Dr.Sumrall visited our campus and made a lasting impression on me. I thought, "If I ever pastor a church I am going to invite him to speak. That day finally came and I was in awe of this great, yet humble, man of God.

The building we were in at that time was small. There were people standing everywhere. We even opened the windows so that people could sit on blankets and hear his anointed preaching.

After the service I took him to a restaurant and bought him the biggest steak on the menu.

During our conversation I confessed, "I'm going to have to increase my faith and get a larger place so that when you return we can accommodate the people."

Dr. Sumrall looked at me and said, "Hmmm," as only he can say it.

Then he paused for a moment and said, "You do not need more faith."

Then Dr. Sumrall continued, "You do not need more faith. You just need to know what faith is."

I could have told him, "Well, I have been to Bible school and can quote Hebrews 11:1 and Mark 11:22-24," but I did not.

He asked, "Do you want to know what faith is?"

"Yes, I do," I replied anxiously.

I scooted to the front edge of my chair and leaned over until my tie was in my steak.

He said, "Faith is . . ." and I took out my pen and began to write. "Faith is . . . simply knowing God."

A light clicked on inside me. Dr. Sumrall didn't say faith was knowing *about* God. He didn't say faith was having a journal full of notes concerning God. He didn't even say that faith was knowing the Bible. He simply stated, "Faith is knowing God."

Since that moment I have been on a quest to know Him.

A Powerful Combination

There are three important factors at work in the process of possession: *faith, belief and prayer.*

First: Have faith.

Jesus tells us to "Have faith in God" (Mark 11:22).

Second: Believe.

In the next verse, the Lord declares, "Whosoever shall say unto this mountain, Be thou removed, and be thou cast into the sea; and shall not doubt in his heart, but shall believe that those things which he saith shall come to pass; he shall have whatsoever he saith" (v. 23).

Third: Pray.

After directing us to have faith and believe, Jesus made this significant statement. "What things soever ye desire, when ye pray, believe that ye receive them, and ye shall have them" (v.24).

When these three elements are combined, they become more powerful than any weapon of war. They can part the waters, cause your enemy to flee, and release God's vast abundance.

The moment you begin to pray with faith and belief, you are no longer looking at what you have, but what you *shall* have. You can say, "It's Monday and I don't have it, but Friday's coming!"

God used "faith talk" when He spoke to the children of Israel. He envisioned a day that was coming: "When thou art come in unto the land which the Lord thy God giveth thee for an inheritance, and possessest it, and dwellest therein" (Deuteronomy 26:1).

Without faith there will be no occupation — no possession.

Earlier, we talked about the necessity of putting on

the whole armor of God. But your battle gear is not complete without prayer. Immediately after the Word tells you to take the helmet of salvation and the sword of the Spirit, we find these words: "Praying always with all prayer and supplication in the Spirit" (Ephesians 6:18).

You may say, "I'm having such a struggle financially I'm doing everything I know to do."

Are you? What would your financial situation be like if you really prayed? How much fasting have you done?

Is it the Word that is not working? Or are you not working the Word?

How does your praying compare with your complaining?

War is hell. Sometimes you are called to the front lines. There are nights you don't get a wink of sleep because you're crouching in a foxhole and the enemy is dropping bombs on all sides.

I asked one man, "How far out of bondage do you want to be."

"Totally," he replied.

"Well, how much of a price are you willing to pay? I asked.

He hesitated. He wasn't sure.

If you truly want to possess the land, here are five things you need to do.

1. Pray with fasting.

Fasting is not a hunger strike against God — trying to persuade Him to do something, or wanting Him to feel sorry for you because you haven't eaten. Instead, it is a denial of self that brings you to a point where you can align your spirit with what God already intends to do.

Jesus explained what it really took for a demon to be totally loosed. He said, "This kind goeth not out but by prayer and fasting" (Matthew 17:21).

2. Pray with intensity.

Have you ever seen a pit bull lock its jaws onto something? They grab so tightly you wonder if they'll ever let go. That's the way we need to storm the gates of heaven. Possessing the land requires calling on God with fervor and passion.

3. Pray with authority.

Elijah didn't take a back seat when he stood on Mount Carmel to call fire down from heaven. He declared, "Lord God of Abraham, Isaac, and of Israel, let it be known this day that thou art God in Israel, and that I am thy servant, and that I have done all these things at thy word" (1 Kings 18:36).

What happened? The fire fell.

Jesus said, "Whatsoever ye shall bind on earth shall

be bound in heaven: and whatsoever ye shall loose on earth shall be loosed in heaven" (Matthew 18:18).

There have been times when I actually laid my hands on my checkbook and prophesied abundance in the name of the Lord.

4. Pray with agreement.

It is impossible to explain the power that is loosed when we pray in one accord. Jesus said, "If two of you shall agree on earth as touching any thing that they shall ask, it shall be done for them of my Father which is in heaven. For where two or three are gathered together in my name, there am I in the midst of them" (Matthew 18:19,20).

Husbands and wives need to be united in their prayer life. Why should we quarrel over the use of God's abundance?

5. Pray in the Spirit.

We don't always know the snares Satan has placed in our paths, but the Holy Spirit does. That's why every Christian needs to know what it means to pray in the Spirit. Do you have a heavenly prayer language?

Paul wrote, "For we know not what we should pray for as we ought: but the Spirit itself maketh intercession for us with groanings which cannot be uttered" (Romans 8:26).

6. Pray with thanksgiving.

Thank God in advance for the land you are about to possess. Praise Him that He is a God of mercy, of grace and of abundance.

"Let us come before his presence with thanksgiving, and make a joyful noise unto him with psalms" (Psalm 95:2).

Dawn is Breaking

You may feel as though you are light years away from moving into God's blessing. You may even feel like poor old Job. Remember him?

He was sitting on an ash heap. His crops were gone. He had lost his cattle, his sheep, even his children.

It was as if the steel mill had shut down, his unemployment benefits had expired and he was no longer eligible for food stamps or a welfare check.

In an act of mercy, Job's wife said, "You're going to die anyway. Why don't you just curse God and get it over with?"

Job replied, "I can't do that."

"Why not?" she wanted to know.

"Well, I know something other people don't know," Job proclaimed. "For I know that my redeemer liveth . . . and though after my skin worms destroy this body, yet in my flesh shall I see God" (Job 19:25,26).

It was midnight, but dawn was about to break. Job may have been in the pit, but he was about to possess a palace.

The Bible says that God not only restored him, but "the Lord gave Job twice as much as he had before" (Job 42:10).

The same God who brought Job back from the jaws of death can also touch your life. He is much closer than you realize.

It's time to tell Satan — that dethroned, defeated, conquered devil — "You have no authority. It's not your territory! I'm taking back what rightfully belongs to me."

It is God's kingdom. He wants the land to be conquered, and He is accomplishing the task through you! "Be strong in the Lord, and in the power of his might" (Ephesians 6:10).

Everything you need is already available because our God is El Shaddai — the one who is all sufficient. Claim it!

GOLDEN KEY #3

THE PROCESS OF PROTECTING YOUR SEED

We live in a disposable society.

From diapers to dishes people go through life throwing things away. After two years we're bored with our cars and trade them in for ones with more "bells and whistles." The Salvation Army and Goodwill thrift stores could hardly exist without people who are constantly discarding their clothing, appliances and furniture.

According to the divorce rates, half of those who make wedding vows break them and toss their mates aside. Today, when couples face the slightest confrontation — such as what television program to watch or where to spend a summer vacation — they begin looking for an exit.

One fellow laughed, "When my wife is forty, I'm going to trade her in for two twenties." All too often it's not a joke.

It happens in church life, too. People develop few roots and flit from congregation to congregation at whim.

God is searching for stability. He always has.

The same verse that tells us to possess the land also tells us to protect it — by physically dwelling on it and becoming long term residents. "When thou art come in unto the land which the Lord thy God giveth thee for an inheritance, and possessest it, and dwellest therein" (Deuteronomy 26:1).

Golden Key #3 involves *the process of protecting your seed.*

The Hebrew word for dwell is *yashab* — which means "to settle into," or "to be secure." It refers to the place where you homestead, marry, set up housekeeping and resist all "claim jumpers."

A Vow of Honor

The favor of God is contingent upon our action.

There are conditions attached. The Lord says, "I will bless you *if* you do what I command."

God declares: "If thou shalt hearken diligently unto the voice of the Lord thy God, to observe and to do all his commandments which I command thee this day, that the Lord thy God will set thee on high above all nations of the earth" (Deuteronomy 28:1).

"If" we protect our seed by dwelling in the land, endless blessings are ours — from an increase in our finances to God's favor on our family.

We must learn to unite ourselves with what the Lord makes available — yes, to become married to it and to make a pledge to honor and obey.

God promised the children of Israel that He would bring them into a new land, but He said, "After you have driven out the inhabitants, taken the spoils, and offered the first fruits to me, I want you to settle down!"

> *The Lord doesn't have a problem transferring the wealth of the wicked into the hands of the righteous.*

He promises, "Ask of me, and I shall give thee the heathen for thine inheritance, and the uttermost parts of the earth for thy possession" (Psalm 2:8).

It's Yours!

When the Lord sees you are serious about planting, He will give you the land to possess. God says, "That land belongs to you." He knows you are investing in your future.

If the land is too crowded, He will give you more.

Lot and Abraham separated because they each needed more territory. "The land was not able to bear them, that they might dwell together: for their substance was great" (Genesis 13:6).

> *God is not worried about how much land you own; He wants to know about your productivity.*

The ancient Hebrews often measured their land by the mount of seed necessary for sowing. Moses said, "If a man shall sanctify unto the Lord some part of a field of his possession, then thy estimation shall be according to the seed thereof" (Leviticus 27:16).

Results are more important than acreage.

72

The Lord not only provides provision, but protection. "Verily, verily, I say unto you, If a man keep my saying, he shall never see death" (John 8:51). The meaning of those words in the original Greek is that we are placed in a position of absolute protection — chaperoned, as a father would protect his virgin daughters.

God will drive off those who would steal the seeds from the land you possess, and protect your field from intruders.

He's right there; concerned about the health of your children; believing with you for a breakthrough in your finances; protecting your marriage.

Highs and Lows

There is no guarantee the task will be easy. You may experience moments of great excitement to hours of deep despair.

The problem of being in the valley is that we think we will be there forever. And when we reach the top of the mountain it's the same. We think we will never come down.

What did God tell His people? "The land, whither ye go to possess it, is a land of hills and valleys" (Deuteronomy 11:11).

We need to realize that circumstances are part of

God's process that brings us into His Promised Land. There are good times and bad. It's much like the vow you make at the wedding altar. You commit yourselves: "For better, for worse, for richer, for poorer, in sickness and in health, as long as you both shall live."

If every moment was a bed of roses, the Word would not have told us to "Rejoice with them that do rejoice, and weep with them that weep" (Romans 12:15).

There will be laughter and tears, but we need to see beyond our limited vision.

> ### *The overall plan of the Father is to prosper us and do us no harm.*

A Kinsman Redeemer

Sowing is a sign of possession.

Even today, in parts of the Middle East, marriages are consummated by the long-held tradition of sowing seed. If no seed is sown there can be an annulment — because they believe in the eyes of God no marriage has occurred.

There's a wonderful story of redemption in the Old Testament. It involves Ruth and Boaz.

When Ruth's husband died, she was still the property of her husband's family. In the land of Moab, the rights and property of a person could only be redeemed by a near relative called a "kinsman redeemer."

Boaz fell in love with Ruth, but there was another near kinsman who had the right, but not the determination, to redeem her.

The kinsman who was unwilling to redeem her took off his sandals, symbolizing his unwillingness to walk on the stony ground. It was a sign that Boaz, in his place, could sow the seed which was necessary to redeem the land of Ruth's dead husband.

> *To take possession and provide protection, you not only need a legal right, you need a sovereign will.*

Once, a man by the name of Onan, one of the sons of Judah, was given an order he refused. He was required to marry the wife of his dead brother and have children, to ensure there would be an inheritance.

Judah requested, "Go into thy brother's wife, and

marry her, and raise up seed to thy brother" (Genesis 38:8).

Because he would not sow the seed, God killed him. Onan also had the right, but not the will, to redeem.

Jesus, unlike the near kinsman or Onan, had both the right and the will to offer redemption.

God was willing to bury the necessary seed in a borrowed tomb. That seed sprang to life and remains alive today. His seed greatly multiplied. Christ was "the firstborn among many brethren" (Romans 8:28).

Planting Peas

There was a man who lived in the time of David by the name of Shammah. He was a pea farmer.

Day after day, Shammah took his hoe and dug trenches in the rocky soil. Then he would take the lentils he used as seed and plant them very carefully.

When the crop began to spring up Shammah watched over it like a caring father. In the heat of the day, he would pull weeds until his back was about to break. Sweat dripped from his face. He tried to conserve the little rain that fell and drove the varmints off the land, saying:

Get out of the way. I've got a harvest coming.

Every year Shammah planted that field, hoping the crop would help feed his family in the winter. But each year, about that same time, he would look up in the noonday sun and see empty wagons coming over the hills. They were the wagons of his adversaries, the Philistines.

Down they would come — clattering, clanking and rumbling down the road. The Philistines would arrive with empty wagons, because they were going to rape his field, harvest his crop and take the spoils back to feed their families.

Peas don't seem too important unless, of course, they are *your* peas.

One day Shammah was toiling in the field. He was practically exhausted when he looked up and there they were!

Hundreds of Philistines headed toward him. He could see their swords gleaming in the sun and their empty wagons ready to be filled.

Scripture records that Shammah "stood in the midst of the ground and defended it" (2 Samuel 23:12).

Shammah had all he could take. He had reached the place where he said, "Enough is enough!"

As the Philistines began to invade, the farmer stuck his hoe in the ground, pointed his finger at the enemy and shouted, "Wait just one minute! You didn't plant one seed on this property. You didn't hoe, you didn't weed and you didn't water." He continued, "I have produced this crop by the sweat of my brow. I'm warning you: don't take one more step on this land."

They laughed in his face and clanged their swords together to intimidate him. Their horses reared up on their back legs and pawed at the air in front of him.

The captain sneered and asked, "Little man, who are you to defy the army of the Philistines?"

He stood tall and with boldness declared, "I am Shammah!"

That name may not mean much to you and me, but it was a word that caused the Philistines to shudder. Shammah is not just any name, but one of the compound titles of Jehovah.

When he said "Shammah!" he spoke of the undeniable, manifested, tangible presence of Jehovah — the Lord of Hosts, the God of battles.

Those plundering Philistines were no longer confronting a lowly farmer with his hoe. Now they were dealing with the champion of the Israelites, the God of heaven and earth. He was there in that field, walking, guarding and protecting. Shammah was there!

The Philistines were defeated. They fled for their lives "and the Lord wrought a great victory" (v.12).

When you plant your crop, the enemy will surely swoop down and attempt to ravage your field and steal your harvest.

> *You can't allow anything to threaten your seed — not people, not opinions, not thoughts, not doubt.*

Jehovah Shammah will stand with you as you tell Satan, "Stop. Don't come one step closer!"

"Get out of my body, devil. Shammah is with me!"

"Get out of my family. Shammah is with me!"

"Get out of my finances. Shammah is with me!"

"Get out of my mind. Shammah is with me!"

Enough is enough!

Hello! Hello!

God knows how to get our attention when He has an important message. He doesn't just call our name once, He calls it twice.

When the Lord wanted to get the prophet's attention, He didn't say "Samuel," but "Samuel, Samuel. Then Samuel answered, Speak; for thy servant heareth" (1 Samuel 3:10).

When God looked for an apostle to write two-thirds of the New Testament, He didn't just say, "Saul." The voice from heaven proclaimed, "Saul, Saul, why persecutest thou me?" (Acts 9:4).

On the Cross, Jesus looked up and said, "My God, my God, why hast thou forsaken me?"(Matthew 27:46).

After the Last Supper, Peter was confronted by the Lord, who said "Simon, Simon, behold, Satan hath desired to have you that he may sift you as wheat" (Luke 22:31). The devil requested and received permission to attack Peter.

Then Jesus added words of great importance. He told the apostle, "But I have prayed for thee, that thy faith fail not" (v.32).

Perhaps you are like Peter. You can't seem to have faith in your faith.

The Lord will place you on His prayer list so that your belief, trust, and hope will not falter.

Why does the Lord pray for us? Because He doesn't want us to lose our spiritual possessions. He was aware that Peter would deny Him three times, but that didn't mean He was giving up on the apostle. No. He knew that one day Peter would preach a revival in Jerusalem that would bring thousands into the kingdom.

When I walk through a valley in my life there is a picture I have of Jesus that I see through the eyes of my spirit. I see Him kneeling at the right hand of the Father — in a position of intercession. He is on one knee with one hand reaching up to hold the hand of God, and the other hand pointing down at me. I see Jesus praying for me.

Let me ask this question. If the Lord is praying for you, how can your faith fail?

Johnny's Pizza

I remember a night my dad and I were out for a drive in the family car. "I could eat a pizza as big as this steering wheel," my father told me.

My eyes lit up. "Pizza?
Can we have a pizza?" I asked.

81

I was only six years old, and we were living on the south side of Columbus, Ohio. It was definitely not one of the best neighborhoods in town. The area had the reputation of being a tavern district.

Both of my parents were working two jobs trying to earn a living, and pizza was a big, big treat for us.

We drove over to Johnny's Pizza, a typical south side hangout. While my dad ordered a pepperoni pizza, I walked over to an area where they had some coin-operated games.

There was one game in particular that intrigued me. It was a miniature bowling alley. You'd slide some little silver disks down a long wooden surface and hit some small buttons under the hanging bowling pins. They'd pop up when the disk hit the buttons.

I was just big enough to put my chin over the side of the game to see what was going on.

I'll never forget the fellow who was playing this particular game. The bearded man had his Harley motorcycle parked outside, and he had tattoos on top of his tattoos. He must have thought someone was going to steal his wallet. It was sticking about four inches out of his back pocket, and there was a big dog chain that tied it to his belt. He had forearms that looked like hams, and he was chomping on a cigar.

There he was, this tough-looking man playing this

bowling game. It seemed a little out of character.

Well, I was just a kid, so when he slid the disk down the board I reached out and grabbed it. I slid it the rest of the way myself.

He just looked at me and sort of growled.

He slid the next disk and I did the same thing again.

Now he was roaring. The mean-looking man marched around the end of the game table and was about to grab me.

Then, in an instant, I felt someone reach around from behind and place an arm across my little chest. It was my father. He saw what was going on and rushed over to protect me.

The man stood there, not saying a word. He was glaring harshly at both of us.

My dad said, "Mister, did you have something to say to the boy? Because if you do, just say it to me. I'm his father."

The angry man just chomped on his cigar, turned around and continued playing his little game.

I've thought about that incident many times.

*More than once, when Satan
has tried to attack, I have
felt the arm of the Galilean
reach out to protect me.*

And like a child I hear the voice of my heavenly Father say to the devil, "If you have anything to say, you're going to have to talk to me!"

A Shield and Buckler

The Lord can provide such protection that even Satan won't know your address. The psalmist wrote: "He that dwelleth in the secret place of the most High shall abide under the shadow of the Almighty" (Psalm 91:1).

You will not only be shielded by the Lord, you will tell others how they can find the same protection.

> "I will say of the Lord,
> He is my refuge and my fortress: my God; in him will I trust.
> Surely he shall deliver thee from the snare of the fowler, and from the noisome pestilence.
> He shall cover thee with his feathers, and under his wing shalt thou trust: his truth shall be

thy shield and buckler" (Psalm 91:2-4).

Satan is not fighting you, he is fighting God. And since you are in God's kingdom, the Lord will guard and protect you. "There shall be no evil befall thee, neither shall any plague come nigh thy dwelling" (v.10) Remember:

- God provides both possession and protection.
- The Lord's favor is contingent on our action.
- What you produce is more important than what you own.
- There may be temporary setbacks, but God's long range plan is for your abundance.
- Never shy away from Satan.

The Lord is your sentry, watching over what He has entrusted to you. By the authority of God you can say, "This land is my land."

TEN GOLDEN KEYS TO YOUR ABUNDANCE

GOLDEN KEY #4

THE PROCESS OF WATERING YOUR SEED

As God began to reveal the keys to His abundance, it was as if I was hit by a thunderbolt. It was not an audible voice from heaven, but by the piercing words I was reading in Scripture.

I said to myself, "Rod Parsley, it has not been working for you. The Bible says you would have more than you could contain and it isn't happening." Then, the Lord showed me that I had not been tithing according to the Word.

At the age of six, when my parents began giving me fifty cents a week as an allowance, they sat me down at the kitchen table and said, "Ten percent of this — one nickel — belongs to the Lord." They read to me the

Scriptures on tithing found in the third chapter of Malachi.

The next Sunday I placed five pennies in the offering plate of the church we attended. Since that day, I have been a faithful tither.

I must admit that in my early years I had plenty of motivation from the pulpit. As a good Baptist boy I knew that if I didn't give to God it would be counted as a sin. I also knew that if I sinned, I would go to a burning hell. And what little boy wants to go to hell — especially when the minister preached hard enough to make me smell the smoke and feel the heat?

Then, many years later God showed me what I am about to share with you regarding tithes and offerings.

Time to Water

Let's begin with a little background.

The children of Israel were told that when they took possession of the land of their inheritance, they were to present their tithe and offerings to the priest "and say unto him, I profess this day unto the Lord thy God..." (Deuteronomy 26:3).

Their seed was to be watered with their profession of faith.

Then the priest was instructed to take the basket

containing their offerings and set it down before the altar of the Lord and give an opportunity for the giver to speak. "And thou shalt speak and say before the Lord thy God . . ." (v.5).

What was the speech they were to give? It was a recounting of their deliverance from bondage.

Their seed was watered by recalling their salvation.

As I carefully read the account from Deuteronomy, what the Lord convicted me of had nothing to do with my mathematics. I was returning to God what was rightfully His. It had to do with the Lord's mandate. My gifts were not accompanied with a profession of faith and a declaration of God's deliverance.

Are you ready to see what you have planted begin to sprout through the soil? Isn't it time for your crops to bear fruit?

Golden Key #4 is vital. You are about to discover the process of watering your seed.

After claiming your inheritance. *After* possessing the land. *After* presenting your gifts to God. It's time to make a declaration — to speak to your seed.

The children of Israel reminded God of four things:

1. They recounted their origin.

Do you remember your beginnings — the place from which the Lord brought you? Those who escaped the bondage of Egypt certainly did. Moses said, "And thou shalt speak and say before the Lord thy God, A Syrian ready to perish was my father, and he went down into Egypt, and sojourned there with a few, and became there a nation, great, mighty, and populous" (Deuteronomy 26:5).

They recalled being beaten by their Egyptian taskmasters for not making enough bricks. And they remembered when God sent a deliverer, by the name of Moses, who was going to lead them out of bondage.

They recounted the plagues that came upon Egypt and how the firstborn of every house was to be killed. But the deliverer said, "If you put a little blood on the doorposts of your house, the death angel will pass over you."

Have you remembered your beginnings? The Bible talks about a "time ye were without Christ, being aliens from the commonwealth of Israel, and strangers from the covenants of promise having no hope, and without God in the world" (Ephesians 2:12). We were plummeting hopelessly and helplessly over the edge of hell's abyss.

That was our condition, and we need to recall it as

we bring our tithes.

2. They recounted their persecution.

Under the rule of Pharaoh, Israel became a nation of slaves. The forced labor they endured "made their lives bitter" (Exodus 1:14). As Moses recalled, "The Egyptians evil entreated us, and afflicted us, and laid upon us hard bondage" (Deuteronomy 26:6).

Talking about your past should not be used as an opportunity to show off your scars, but as a time to speak with humility about your experiences.

It's all right to remember.

Think about the battles of the past. "Call to remembrance the former days, in which, after ye were illuminated, ye endured a great fight of afflictions" (Hebrews 10:32).

The devil is the number one proponent of child abuse. He exploits and torments his children. He does not love you and never has.

Satan is only interested in your persecution. And since you were born in the image of God, he wants to mar that image. Since he can't harm God, he injures and wounds God's creation.

91

3. They recounted their deliverance.

This was a time to say, "Look what the Lord has done." Egypt was behind them. They had been redeemed.

Now they could praise the Almighty, saying, "And when we cried unto the Lord God of our fathers, the Lord heard our voice, and looked on our affliction. and our labour, and oppression: And the Lord brought us forth out of Egypt with a mighty hand, and with an outstretched arm" (Deuteronomy 26: 7,8).

Dozens of times in Scripture God is referred to as having strength and power in His arm. As the psalmist wrote, "Thou hast a mighty arm . . . and high is thy right hand" (Psalm 89:13).

The finger of the Lord created the heavens (Psalm 8:3). The hand of the Lord created the earth (Psalm 95:5). But it was the strong right arm of the Lord that brought deliverance (Deuteronomy 26:8).

David was only a shepherd boy, but he gained faith be recalling past victories. When he was about to face mighty Goliath, he told a worried King Saul, "Thy servant slew both the lion and the bear: and this uncircumcised Philistine shall be as one of them" (1 Samuel 17:36).

You are watering your seed when you remind the Lord of how He delivered you.

4. They recounted their possession of the land.

Finally, the Israelites could thank God and declare, "He hath brought us into this place, and hath given us this land, even a land that floweth with milk and honey. And now, behold, I have brought the first fruits of the land, which thou, O Lord, hast given me. And thou shalt set it before the Lord thy God, and worship before the Lord thy God: And thou shalt rejoice in every good thing which the Lord thy God hath given unto thee, and unto thine house" (vv.9-11).

Filthy Rags

We need to remember who we were, where we were and what we were before God found us.

You can dress a woman in a $1 million mink coat, put diamonds on her fingers, put $1,000-an-ounce perfume behind her ears, and place her in a $150,000 automobile; but underneath the facade, she's still just sinful flesh. That's what we all are. Our righteousness is "as filthy rags" (Isaiah 64:6).

As sinners we are reprehensible, disgusting and vile. If left to our own devices, we will destroy not only ourselves, but everything else around us.

Years ago I heard a minister say:

Only when you see the magnitude of your sin, will you see the magnitude of His righteousness.

There comes a time when we need to recognize our present state: We are sinners in need of a Savior.

Jesus told the Pharisees, "They that be whole need not a physician, but they that are sick" (Matthew 9:12). Then He explained, "I am not come to call the righteous, but sinners to repentance" (v.13).

The Israelites had done very little to receive the Lord's delivering power. Yes, they endured bondage, but God had a plan for their redemption that centered on something they did not understand. It was called grace.

Everything we have is the result of the mercy of God. I like the way Vance Havner presents it in his book, *Truth for Each Day:*

> G stands for gift, the principle of grace.
> R stands for redemption, the purpose of grace.
> A stands for access, the privilege of grace.
> C stands for character, the product of grace.
> E stands for eternal life, the prospect of grace.

The Lord's unmerited favor is provided free. And

there are no "works" you can do to receive it. Grace is a free gift of God.

A Grand Entrance

If you want your lands to be filled with God's abundance, there are two necessary steps. They are as essential as water and sunshine.

1. Believe with your heart.
2. Confess with your mouth.

Those two elements are at the center of the message Paul gave to the Christians at Rome. He declared: "The word is nigh thee, even in thy mouth, and in thy heart: that is, the word of faith, which we preach; That if thou shalt confess with thy mouth the Lord Jesus, and shalt believe in thine heart that God hath raised him from the dead, thou shalt be saved. For with the heart man believeth unto righteousness; and with the mouth confession is made unto salvation" (Romans 10:8-10).

How does faith and belief enter our hearts? They make their entrance through the Word. Paul wrote, "So faith cometh by hearing, and hearing by the word of God" (Romans 10:17).

It doesn't take a theologian to figure out that faith comes by listening to the prophetic Word of God.

When you hear the Word, it builds faith. And when your faith is built, it produces belief. And belief allows you to speak. When you speak, your faith-filled words tap into the life-changing power of God.

Jesus said, "Whatsoever ye shall ask in my name, that will I do that the Father may be glorified in the Son" (John 14:13).

A lack of understanding will keep you in bondage — both spiritually and financially.

God doesn't want us to walk without knowledge, "Having the understanding darkened, being alienated from the life of God through . . . ignorance..." (Ephesians 4:18).

When we receive the right information, a chain reaction is triggered that leads to good things:

- Information leads to knowledge.
- Knowledge leads to understanding.
- Understanding leads to trust.
- Trust leads to faith.
- Faith leads to belief.

It was the apostle Paul who wrote, "For whosoever

shall call upon the name of the Lord shall be saved" (Romans 10:13).

Then he asked a series of questions that is at the heart of faith, belief, and evangelism. He wanted to know, "How then shall they call on him in whom they have not believed? and how shall they believe in him of whom they have not heard? and how shall they hear without a preacher? And how shall they preach, except they be sent?" (Romans 10:14,15).

It begins with hearing the voice of the Lord.

Your first step on this journey begins with a preacher — a prophetic voice. As a minister of the Gospel, when I deliver the Word, someone can *hear* the Word and *believe* the Word. Then, and only then, are they ready for the next step. Now they can "call upon the name of the Lord and be saved."

Abundance is not the result of simply asking. There are prerequisites involved.

Don't attempt to speak before you listen. Otherwise you will have no trust, confidence and faith.

There are people who see a luxury automobile and immediately say, "I claim that car. I receive that car in the name of the Lord!"

Well, you can say those words until your tongue falls out; it won't make any difference.

You don't speak so you can believe. Belief must come first. What about hearing a prophetic word? What about God's will in the matter?

Salvation comes when we first believe it and then confess it.

Healing comes when we believe in our hearts and confess with our mouths, "By your stripes I am healed."

When Paul was preaching in a place called Lystra, a man who had been crippled from birth was brought to him. The man "heard Paul speak" (Acts 14:9).

What started with listening ended with leaping. Scripture records that Paul looked at the man: "and perceiving that he had faith to be healed, Said with a loud voice, Stand upright on thy feet. And he leaped and walked" (vv.9,10).

Giant Faith!

I believe in exercise because I have seen its results. And I'm talking about more than doing push-ups or lifting weights. God expects us to exercise our faith.

Ten years ago I had $100,000 faith. Then it became $300,000 faith, then a half million and $1 million.

Today my faith has exceeded $2 million.

Why has my faith increased? Because I have seen

offerings that size given to this ministry.

I didn't start with million-dollar faith. I couldn't count that high. God took me from where I was to where He wanted me to be.

When we read about the miracles of Jesus, it was *hearing* that produced such great faith. "But so much the more went there a fame abroad about him: and great multitudes came together to hear, and to be healed by him of their infirmities" (Luke 5:15).

The purpose of hearing and understanding is so that we will have faith to believe.

During the ministry of Jesus, a man wanted the Lord to heal his son who had a spirit that had robbed him of his speech. "And wheresoever he taketh him, he teareth him: and he foameth, and gnasheth with his teeth, and pineth away" (Mark 9:18).

Jesus said, "Bring him unto me" (v.19).

When they brought the boy forward, the foul spirit immediately threw the boy into a convulsion. "He fell on the ground, and wallowed foaming" (v.20).

Jesus asked the boy's father, "How long is it since this came unto him?" (v.21).

The father answered that his son had the condition since he was a little child.

Jesus said to the man, "If thou canst believe, all things are possible to him that believeth" (v.23).

It was not a question of whether or not Christ could perform a miracle. It was a question of belief.

As a result of what the Lord had spoken, "The father of the child cried out, and said with tears, Lord I believe; help thou mine unbelief" (v.24).

Christ rebuked the evil spirit, saying, "Thou dumb and deaf spirit, I charge thee, come out of him, and enter no more into him" (v.25).

The spirit shrieked and violently convulsed in the boy and then came out. The crowd that had gathered thought he had died. "But Jesus took him by the hand, and lifted him up; and he arose" (v.27).

Do you remember the story of the woman who came to Jesus with an issue of blood? After living with the condition for twelve years, she said to herself, "If I may but touch his garment, I shall be whole" (Matthew 9:21).

She was filled with belief. In her heart she was saying, "I know I can, I know I can."

The woman was healed because she heard, she spoke, and she believed.

The Missing Link

What should you do when you have a gigantic problem? Speak to it! When your words are combined with your faith, miracles happen. What did Jesus say? "Whosoever shall say unto this mountain. Be thou removed . . and shall not doubt in his heart, but shall believe . . . he shall have whatsoever he saith" (Mark 11:23).

For years I had been taught that belief is all that matters. Now I know that faith must be linked with confession.

Believing with your heart and speaking with your mouth are the two hinges on which the door of abundance swings.

I've met some people who believe the Bible teaches that whatever we ask we can have — with no strings attached. They obviously have not read the words of John. He wrote, "And this is the confidence that we have in him, that, if we ask any thing according to his will, he heareth us" (1 John 5:14).

We can't ask outside the will of God and expect an answer. But when our request lines up with His will, we have the guarantee that He will not only hear us, but that the answer is on the way. It is already accomplished.

The twenty-sixth chapter of Deuteronomy contains all the keys to abundance I am sharing in this book. It is interesting that in these passages, Moses spent more time dealing with the confession of the mouths of the Israelites than any other subject.

Your words become the vehicle that carries you out of bondage and into the land of abundance.

Seeing the Invisible

At this very moment God is at work on your behalf. As I told someone, "He may be arranging to have you fired from your job. Why? Because He knows that unless that happens you will never move to the position He has prepared for you that is more than you ever dreamed."

Oppression and persecution are often the opportunity for advancement. Joseph would have never made it to the palace if he had not been working in the prison.

The Lord sees the end before the beginning. One day Jesus was teaching in a synagogue and there was a woman who had a spirit of infirmity for eighteen years. She "was bowed together, and could in no wise lift up herself" (Luke 13:11).

When the Lord saw her, He called her over to Him and said, "Woman, thou art loosed from thine infirmity" (v.12).

You say, "How could He make such a statement? She wasn't yet healed. At that moment she was still bent over."

To the Lord, her healing had already happened. In His eyes, she was made whole and He saw her in a totally different dimension. It was after Christ saw her as healed that "He laid his hands on her: and immediately she was made straight, and glorified God" (v.13).

Start seeing your situation as completed. To God it is not a promise, but a fact.

Hear His prophetic word, believe it, speak it and accept it.

When you do, you will be able to say, like Paul, "We are troubled on every side, yet not distressed; we are perplexed, but not in despair; Persecuted, but not forsaken; cast down, but not destroyed" (2 Corinthians 4:8,9).

You will be able to declare, "Having the same spirit of faith . . . I believed, and therefore have I spoken; we also believe, and therefore speak" (2 Corinthians 4:13).

Your words are the "release valve" of faith. Hope and expectation will never rise above your level of confession.

What you are speaking is what you are believing. Jesus, talking about those things which are deep within a man, said, "Out of the abundance of the heart his mouth speaketh" (Luke 6:45).

Are you speaking to your seed?

- "Death and life are in the power of the tongue" (Proverbs 18:21).
- "For by thy words thou shalt be justified, and by thy words thou shalt be condemned" (Matthew 12:37).
- Jesus said, "The words that I speak unto you, they are spirit and they are life" (John 6:63).

Blossoms in Winter

When Paul was chained to the walls of the sewer systems of Rome, he declared, "Wherein I suffer trouble, as an evildoer, even unto bonds; but the word of God is not bound" (2 Timothy 2:9).

Paul knew deep inside that when he spoke the Word, there were no chains that could keep his body down.

We will reap tomorrow the seeds of the words we

sow today. If they have been released from a heart full of faith and belief, get ready for your barns to overflow.

The Lord asked Jeremiah, "What do you see?"

The prophet responded, "I see a rod of an almond tree" (Jeremiah 1:11). He saw it blossoming and bearing fruit in the middle of winter.

The Lord replied, "Thou has well seen: for I will hasten my word to perform it" (v.12).

Why do we offer sacrifices of praise to God?

When the fruit of our lips gives thanks to His name, He gives abundance that never ends — winter, spring, summer and fall.

The process of watering your seed includes faith, belief and confession. Never forget your beginnings. Talk with the Lord about those days in your spiritual Egypt when your back was against the wall and Satan was breathing down your neck.

God had a plan for you then and He has one for you now. He has promised never to leave you or forsake you (Hebrews 13:5).

There will always be water for your seed.

Jesus told the woman of Samaria, "Whosoever drinketh of this water shall thirst again: But whosoever drinketh of the water that I shall give him shall never thirst; but the water that I shall give him shall be in him a well of water springing up into everlasting life" (John 4:13,14).

Praise God for the fact that your soil is being watered. Your harvest is on the way.

GOLDEN KEY #5

THE PROCESS OF SELECTING YOUR SOIL

"I don't know where to go to church and I'm so confused as to what ministries I should be supporting," a man confided to me after one of our services in Pennsylvania.

I couldn't blame him. With new congregations springing up like daisies and Christian television programs asking for money about every twenty-two seconds, I'd be baffled, too.

The Golden Key I am about to share with you is a guideline for planting your harvest. You need to know:

- How to determine the signs of good soil.
- How to measure the merits of a ministry.
- How to thwart the attack of demons.

- Why the signs and the gifts are inseparable.
- Why the gift of healing and the gift of tongues were given.

Here is what God says about being soil selective. He instructed Moses to tell the children of Israel that when they came into the land He was giving them, they should bring their first fruits "unto the place which the Lord thy God shall choose to place his name there" (Deuteronomy 26:2).

> *The soil you are seeking is not one that bears a man's name, but a location God Himself has endorsed — a place He has given His name.*

If you want to know how important soil is to seed, just visit the local office of the state agriculture bureau. They'll tell you more about soil than you ever wanted to know — its pH value, its alkaline content, its acidity, and whether it needs more nitrogen, phosphorus or potassium.

One thing is certain. Without good earth you won't have a harvest. You can sow all the seed you want on a carpet and it's not going to grow.

Jesus related the story of the sower whose seed was planted in four different types of ground, but only one of the four produced a harvest. That's only a twenty-five percent success rate.

The seed that was planted along the wayside, on stony ground, and among the thorns failed to produce. The remaining seed was planted in "good ground, and did yield fruit that sprang up and increased" (Mark 4:8).

Five Signs of Good Soil

You may say, "I know that I am to sow seed where God has placed His name, but how can I determine that location?"

The Lord not only makes the answer clear, He has created indicators for us to follow. Here are the five guideposts to look for.

Sign number one: They preach a Gospel of salvation.

You can know immediately if God approves of the location you select for sowing by asking, "Is the Gospel being preached in this place?"

Christ gave us the Great Commission — that we should go into all the world and preach the Gospel to every creature. Then He gave the *message* that is to be preached: "He that believeth and is baptized shall be saved; but he that believeth not shall be damned" (Mark 16:16).

The Lord didn't command for us to go into all the world and solve every human problem we can find. He declared: "Preach the Gospel."

There is nothing wrong in feeding starving children or building clinics in the jungle — in fact we prayerfully support many such efforts. But if that is not combined with an effort to win the lost to Christ we are misinterpreting what God's Word is all about.

Support a ministry that preaches:

- The reality of heaven and hell.
- The cross of Christ.
- Redemption through the blood.
- Healing through the atonement.
- The second coming of Christ.

You can know that your seed is being sown in good soil if there is a strong conviction of right and wrong, and the leadership is not afraid to preach about a three letter word called "sin."

Find a ministry that firmly believes in separation from the world. "Wherefore come out from among them, and be ye separate, saith the Lord" (2 Corinthians 6:17).

Here's another "soil testing" question to ask: "Is the

Gospel that is being preached, the Gospel of the kingdom?"

Much of what is being proclaimed from the pulpits has strayed far from that mandate. Jesus said, "This gospel of the kingdom shall be preached in all the world for a witness unto all nations; and then shall the end come" (Matthew 24:14).

Christ said "This Gospel," not another gospel. It's a problem that has plagued the church since its inception. Paul warned the church at Corinth, "For if he that cometh preacheth another Jesus, whom we have not preached, or if ye receive another spirit, which ye have not received, or another gospel, which ye have not accepted," do not tolerate it! (2 Corinthians 11:4).

Sowing seeds into so-called ministries that are not based on the Gospel is not being soil selective — and you can't be guaranteed a harvest.

If you're not concerned with reaping, then scatter your seed wherever you please — it really doesn't matter. You may just want to help a few nice people. That's fine. But if you want to experience God's abundance, start planting in a place where someone has their sleeves rolled up and is working for the kingdom. Find a church where their sword is not just being polished, but is dripping with the blood of the enemy — where it has pierced the heart and soul of the demonic forces of hell. Get involved with those who are in the heat of the battle.

Immediately following Christ's command to take the Gospel to the world, He declared, "And these signs shall follow them that believe; In my name shall they cast out devils; they shall speak with new tongues; They shall take up serpents; and if they drink any deadly thing, it shall not hurt them; shall they lay hands on the sick, and they shall recover" (Mark 16:17,18).

Sign number two: They shall cast out devils.

This one directive eliminates about ninety percent of the ministries in operation today.

The Word doesn't tell us to counsel demons out of people or to make an appointment for them to see a doctor of psychiatry. The Lord says, "They shall cast out devils."

In most churches this directive is never practiced because the leaders of the church refuse to acknowledge the existence of demons. How can they be cast out if their reality is ignored?

To deny the existence of devils is to deny the existence of angels — and the existence of God.

The basic dilemma in America is not the need for

economic, social, or political reform. The problem is not in Washington, D.C, on Wall Street or with your next door neighbor. Our difficulties stem from one basic cause: *There's a devil loose!*

Why do we have problems with attitudes, allegiances, and attire? *There's a devil loose!*

Why do we have a crisis in our families and our finances? *There's a devil loose!*

I thank God every day that the Bible tells us how to take charge of the enemy. When a boy who was possessed by a demon was brought to Jesus, He rebuked the devil and said, "Come out!" (Mark 9:25). The boy was set free.

"Well, we don't do that in our services," one Pentecostal minister reluctantly told me. "If we deal with the issue at all, it is in private."

> ## *According to the Bible I read, casting out devils is a ministry that is to accompany those who are fulfilling the Great Commission.* (Mark 16:17,18).

Jesus said, "Whosoever shall be ashamed of me and of my words, of him shall the Son of man be ashamed" (Luke 9:26).

I don't care if I am in a coliseum or on national television. I'm not going to soft-soap the Gospel. If we

TEN GOLDEN KEYS TO YOUR ABUNDANCE

cast out devils and speak in tongues in our church, we should not hide it from the world. "For I am not ashamed of the gospel of Christ: for it is the power of God unto salvation" (Romans 1:16).

It's time to lift the veil and let the world see a Spirit-filled ministry in action so they can be delivered from the roaring lion who prowls and stalks the earth.

Where should you sow your seed? In a church that is not afraid of standing up to Satan.

Sign number three: They shall speak with new tongues.

God places His name on a ministry that believes in the baptism of the Holy Spirit.

The Spirit was not only promised; it was delivered. On the day of Pentecost, one hundred and twenty believers gathered in the Upper Room in Jerusalem. Suddenly there came a sound from heaven like a mighty rushing wind that filled the house where they were sitting. "And there appeared unto them cloven tongues like as of fire, and it sat upon each of them. And they were all filled with the Holy Ghost, and began to speak with other tongues, as the Spirit gave them utterance" (Acts 2:3,4).

They received one of the nine gifts that are to be in operation in our life and ministry. The gifts of the Spirit are (1 Corinthians 12:8-10):

1. The word of wisdom.
2. The word of knowledge.
3. Faith.
4. The gifts of healing.
5. The working of miracles.
6. Prophecy.
7. Discerning of spirits.
8. Different kinds of tongues.
9. Interpretation of tongues.

I believe that these nine gifts are linked together in a way that makes them inseparable. Let me explain.

- If you believe in the baptism of the Holy Spirit, you have to believe in speaking in other tongues.
- If you believe in speaking in other tongues, you have to believe in the interpretation of tongues.
- If you believe both in tongues and their interpretation, you have to believe in prophecy because that is what those two gifts produce.
- If you believe in prophecy, you must believe in the "revelation gifts": the discerning of spirits, the word of knowledge and the word of wisdom.
- If you believe in the revelation gifts, then you must believe in the gifts of healing.
- If you believe in the gifts of healing, then you must believe in the supernatural impartation of

the gift of faith.
- If you believe in the gift of faith, you must believe in the working of miracles.

What is my conclusion? A church that believes in the baptism of the Holy Spirit will embrace the gifts of the Spirit — all nine of them. It will also be a ministry where God chooses to place His name.

I am deeply troubled when I know that sincere Christians are sowing into religious organizations that have stated, "Speaking in tongues is of the devil." Oh, they may not widely broadcast that fact, but it is at the core of their doctrine.

Here's what Jesus declared: "All manner of sin and blasphemy shall be forgiven unto men: but the blasphemy against the Holy Ghost shall not be forgiven unto men. And whosoever speaketh a word against the Son of man, it shall be forgiven him; but whosoever speaketh against the Holy Ghost, it shall not be forgiven him, neither in this world, neither in the world to come" (Matthew 12:31,32).

Blasphemy means to speak a word willfully and hurtfully against the Holy Spirit — or to attribute the works of God to the devil.

Be careful. You can scatter seed in any field you desire, but I only want to plant where God has placed His name.

Sign number four: They shall take up serpents; and if they drink any deadly thing, it shall not hurt them.

Being from an eastern Kentucky family, I know more than a little about churches that believe in snake handling.

I heard about a gospel singer and his wife who were invited to sing at a rural mountain church. To their surprise, while they were on the platform, the pastor brought out a box of serpents. The singer turned to his wife and whispered, "Don't worry, honey. Just look around for the back door."

She nervously replied, "I already did and there isn't one."

He grinned and said, "I wonder where they want one?"

A woman took one of the snakes out of the box and started to hand it to the guest. When he took a step back, she asked, "You mean to tell me if the Lord told you to take up a serpent you wouldn't?"

He looked at her and answered, "No ma'am. He hasn't and I'm not."

I've been asked many times, "What does this Scripture deal with? Are we really supposed to physically handle serpents and drink deadly poison?"

My Bible declares, "Thou shalt not tempt the Lord thy God" (Matthew 4:7).

The Word does not contradict itself. When Jesus said "They shall take up serpents," He was not asking us to tempt the Lord, but to boldly take on Satan and his evil works.

Invading Satan's Camp

In my ministry we have "taken on" Satan many times.

Once, for several weeks, we picketed a movie theater that showed X-rated films in an affluent neighborhood of our city.

One night we took a television camera with us — just a camera with no film — to put the fear of God into those who would frequent such an establishment.

That evening a man, who didn't know we were there, walked out of the theater and was frightened beyond words. He exclaimed, "If my wife ever sees this she'll divorce me. If my boss sees this I'll lose my job."

Then he offered to pay any price for the video he thought we were shooting.

Deeply ashamed, the man began to weep like a little child. "I was raised in the church, but this thing has a hold on me," he admitted.

One of the men from our congregation told him, "Sir, it can lose its hold on you." The Christians who were gathered there laid hands on him and cast out the unclean and evil spirits that had him bound to pornography.

The man knelt on the street and gave his heart to Christ.

Later, that establishment sued our church and its individual members for a total of over $11 million. Since pornography is illegal in Ohio, the basis for their argument was that they were involved in "legal adult entertainment" and we were harassing them.

When the case came to court, one of the first witnesses was a cashier who was on duty one of the nights we picketed. The attorney for the prosecution asked her, "What is it that you sell at your establishment?"

"Oh, it's pornography," she blurted out.

"Objection!" yelled the attorney.

The judge said, "You can't object to your own witness."

When another man giving testimony was asked, "How have you been harassed?" he replied, "They told me Jesus loved me."

They even tried to say we were assaulting people because in our literature we stated that we were "loosing an assault on the kingdom of darkness."

The judge didn't buy the argument. He said, "At one time or another we've all probably sung, 'Onward Christian Soldiers.'"

The courts not only ruled in our favor, but the case set a precedent for legally picketing pornographic movie theaters nationwide.

We refuse to be intimidated. We won't back away from Satan.

When a local homosexual and lesbian organization decided to set up an information booth at the Ohio State Fairground, we protested. A seven-year-old girl in our church had been given a piece of their literature that contained graphic descriptions and photographs of how to have so-called "safe sex."

I called every newspaper and every broadcast news department in town and said, "Meet me at the governor's office." When the press gathered, I knocked on his door, but there was no response. So I stood in front of the office and said, "I'm here to tell you that the people of this city and of this state are not ready to tolerate this kind of perversion at a facility that is paid for by the tax dollars of the citizens. We demand that this organization be removed from the State Fairgrounds."

Within two hours the homosexual and lesbian group packed up and disappeared.

Where should you sow? In a place that refuses to back down to Satan.

Sign number five: They shall lay hands on the sick and they shall recover.

Are you investing in a ministry that believes God still heals today? You'd be shocked to learn how many noted leaders believe that miracles ended with the apostles. The only reason they pray for people is to give comfort to the family, not with the belief that God responds to our faith.

Perhaps I am missing something, but my Bible declares: "These signs shall follow them that believe." That's me! I believe!

What's more, I know God heals today because I've witnessed miracles with my own eyes countless times. And the man with an experience is never at the mercy of a man with an argument.

The same Jesus who healed the woman with an issue of blood, who cleansed ten lepers in Samaria, who opened the eyes of blind Bartimaeus, who restored a shriveled hand and healed all manner of sickness and disease, *has the same power today*. He is still in the healing business.

Where are you planting your seed? It needs to be a place that prays for healing according to the Word.

"Is any sick among you? let him call for the elders of
the church; and let them pray over him, anointing
him with oil in the name of the Lord: And the prayer
of faith shall save the sick, and the Lord shall raise
him up" (James 5:14,15).

That's what you'll find in a church that bears the
name of the Lord.

Start Planting

The finest seed in the world will fail if it is not
watered by the Word and nourished by the Spirit.
Sow where there is a continual, tangible presence of
the Lord, and where you can feel the touch of God.

Scripture declares that in the last days there will be
those, "Having a form of godliness, but denying the
power thereof; from such turn away" (2 Timothy
3:5).

When you sow selectively in soil that is approved
by God, He guarantees a bountiful harvest.

GOLDEN KEY #6

TAKE YOUR OFFERING TO THE PRIEST

I'm always amazed when I hear people boast about their giving. They brag, "I pay my tithe every week." Or, "I always give my money to the Lord."

They have it totally backward. It's not *their* money. It's God's. Not just the tithe — all of it."

Every dollar, every dime and every penny is His. The shirt on your back, the shoes on your feet, your beautiful home, your shiny car; it all belongs to the Lord.

The giving is done by God. Because of His great goodness, He allows us to keep ninety percent of what passes through our hands and only asks that we return ten percent to Him — the original owner. Everything else we give is an offering to say "Thank you" to the Lord.

What does the Bible tell us to do with our tithe and our offerings? "And thou shalt go unto the priest that shall be in those days, and say unto him, I profess this day unto the Lord thy God, that I am come unto the country which the Lord sware unto our fathers for to give us. And the priest shall take the basket out of thine hand, and set it down before the altar of the Lord thy God" (Deuteronomy 26:3,4).

That's Golden Key #6: You must take your offering to the priest.

Whose Money Is It?

People who believe they are putting "their" money in the offering plate want to maintain permanent control of it. They say they are giving to the Lord, but place the priest under a microscope regarding its use, wanting to be the permanent guardian.

I constantly remind my congregation, "It's God's money before you ever give it." And once given, it is not the priest's money either. Just because the man of God is accountable for what you present, that doesn't change the ownership. The resources have always belonged to the Almighty.

Do we need accountability in the pulpit? Yes. At the same time we need the same accountability in the pew. I raised a few eyebrows one Sunday morning when I said, "If you demand to know what the preacher is doing with God's money, maybe the preacher needs to know what *you* are doing with God's money."

> *Somehow we need to break the mindset that we are giving to men. No. We are returning to God what is already His.*

There are people who need to sign up for the course "Giving to God 101." They don't understand the first thing about spiritual economics.

What did Moses tell the people? They were to bring their first fruits "to the priest that shall be in those days" (Deuteronomy 26:3). An accurate translation says, "The priest that shall hold the office in those particular days."

I've heard individuals threaten, "I'm not giving my money to that preacher!"

You do not give *to* a priest, you give *through* a priest. The money is not presented to a man, but through a man.

Jesus said, "No man cometh unto the father, but by me," (John 14:6). Why did He say that? He was our priest — and He was our prophet.

The priest's assignment is to take you to God. The

prophet's job is to bring God to you. That's the reason the Bible says that a man is not only the priest of his home, but also the prophet of his home. As the priest, he has the responsibility of bringing his family to God; and as a prophet, he has an obligation to bring God to his family.

The only way to approach the Lord for the forgiveness of sin is through our Priest. His name is Jesus. "Wherefore, holy brethren, partakers of the heavenly calling, consider the Apostle and High Priest of our profession, Christ Jesus" (Hebrews 3:1).

Have you personally seen the Lord today? Have you physically touched Him? Is He standing at the front of the sanctuary to receive the offering you bring on Sunday morning? No. Christ ascended to heaven and entered the Holy of Holies. He sits at the right hand of God making intercession for you and me.

Offices on Earth

Christ is our High Priest, but He has designated and ordained His representatives on earth. He has set them in office according to the fivefold ministry, or offices He has established. "And he gave some, apostles; and some, prophets; and some, evangelists; and some, pastors and teachers" (Ephesians 4:11).

These continue to be the ministries we have today that represent our High Priest, Jesus.

126

To the Lord, the office is much more important than the officeholder.

What is an office? It is the place where the work is done. The Lord has commanded that we bring our first fruits "unto the place which the Lord thy God shall choose to place his name" (Deuteronomy 26:2). He did that when He established the five offices in His Word.

Let me pose a question. Is Ronald Reagan the President of the United States? Is George Bush the President? No. Those men are no longer in office.

The person who occupies the White House only *functions in* the office of the president. He has been given the constitutional authority to function in that role. The office is far more powerful than the man.

When God established His work on earth, He didn't establish men, He established offices.

The Lord ordains a person to hold a particular place of responsibility and gives them this charge: "I am not only giving you the authority of this office, but also the responsibility."

People need to realize that the man or woman God appoints is not an agent of man, but an agent of the Lord. They don't answer to man, but to God.

Since the Lord has placed the minister in authority, we give through that office to the High Priest. That is

127

God's declared plan, but somehow people don't want to accept it.

Called and Chosen

I've talked with numerous ministers who tell me, "I have Mr. 'Big Bucks' on our board, and he is only here because he has money — not because he is called by God or has any spiritual maturity. It's causing havoc in our ministry."

When we have people making decisions without having accountability and responsibility to God, we are placing ourselves in jepoardy.

Just because someone can run a major corporation doesn't mean he knows anything about how the flock of God functions. I believe in organizational skills and savvy business practices, but only when they are in the hands of someone who has been called and chosen by the Lord.

Every deacon, elder and
trustee of the church needs to
be called of God, anointed by the
Holy Spirit, and performing their
task as ministry unto the Lord.

I remember the day, as a teenager, a teacher in my high school took me aside and said, "Rodney, you need to think about going to vocational school. I think you'd be best at working with your hands." It was her polite way of telling me that she didn't think I had the brainpower to make it in the world of business or administration.

Later, in Bible college, one of my professors was even more blunt. He shook his head and said, "Do us a favor. Don't try to start a church. You'll be the biggest embarrassment ever to come out of this school."

Those teachers would have never believed it if someone had told them that one day I would be the pastor of the 5000 seat World Harvest Church, and seen daily on over 14,000 TV stations and cable systems in the United States and Canada.

People don't understand that when you have been chosen by the Lord to hold an office in His kingdom, an astounding thing happens.

He gives you not only the authority and the responsibility, but supplies the knowledge, understanding, wisdom and skills necessary to perform the task.

I don't mind confessing that I have to totally rely on the Holy Spirit every day. If the decisions I'm called on to make came only from Rod Parsley, this ministry would be like a ship without a compass. I constantly need God's guidance and direction.

It is serious business when God appoints you to an office. He says, "You're responsible because I've given you the responsibility. You are accountable because it goes with the office."

It's Not Your Choice

When God's money leaves your hand, the transaction is finished. You've given it "where God has placed His name," and your work is completed. The priest — the office holder — now has the burden. The accountability for those funds is no longer yours, but his.

Some people are upset because they give $22 in an offering and then see the Outreach Ministry with a new van they didn't think was the right choice.

Let me say it one more time: "It's not your problem. You're not accountable, because the responsibility for those decisions is no longer yours!"

There's no need to analyze, evaluate and second-guess the judgment of the office holder. That person answers directly to God. I love the words of an old chorus:

> *Trust and obey,*
> *For there's no other way.*
> *To be happy in Jesus;*
> *But to trust and obey.*

God doesn't tell us to "Figure it out," He says, "Go!" He didn't tell Joshua, "Get out your calculators and physics books to see what combination of pitch and vibration we need to make these walls of Jericho fall down." He said, "March! and blow those horns!"

To whom did God first give those orders? To Joshua, because that's who He had placed in the office.

You may not particularly like the "Joshua" God has chosen as your priest, but it's not your kingdom. You didn't choose the minister, the Lord did.

The apostle Paul could handle the onslaught of Satan; it was caring for the sheep that often gave him distress.

When God gave me the decision-making responsi bility of a large congregation, I didn't shout, "Hallelujah! I wept like a child.

Every Christian needs to learn what they teach at West Point or at the U.S. Naval Academy:

You don't salute the man, you salute his uniform. And the more "stripes" he wears, the greater esteem the uniform deserves.

It makes no difference whether you like his looks, his style, or his orders. He holds the office, and you are to demonstrate your loyalty and respect to that office.

Giving Millions

Abraham, the original seed of the entire nation of Israel, was returning from a lengthy series of battles when he met Melchisedec, the king of Salem, and priest of the most high God.

We have no record that the two men had ever met before this moment — or that they knew anything about each other. When they met, Abraham, with his seed, said to Melchisedec without hesitation, "Here's my tithe." Scripture states, "Now consider how great this man was, unto whom even the patriarch Abraham gave the tenth of the spoils" (Hebrews 7:4).

What Abraham presented was not a small bounty. It wasn't just $10 or $15, but possessions worth millions. He had defeated five kings and their kingdoms. Now he was presenting the tithe to a man he had never seen before. Furthermore, Abraham had no idea how the priest was going to use the funds.

Abraham didn't question, "What are you going to do with the bounty from this victory? Are you going to buy a new bus for our Outreach Ministry? Are you going to air condition the nursery, or pay the utility bill?"

That was not Abraham's responsibility. He was only told to obey.

A Touchy Topic

The minister of a church I once visited, said, "Could you talk to the people about tithing?"

"Don't you teach on tithing?" I asked, rather startled.

"Oh, I don't address that issue directly," he responded. "You know, people are so touchy about that topic."

I shared with him the fact that God's commandment to receive the tithes is no different than the commandment not to commit adultery. It's an order from above.

Presenting your offering to the priest who is currently in office should be as natural as saying "Amen" in church. It's an ordinance established by the Lord much like water baptism.

When we obey in the natural, something transpires in the realm of the supernatural.

The priest to whom you hand God's tithe and your offering is temporary, but in the Lord's sight, the spirit of that office is eternal. The priest accepts what you

133

present and turns it over to the Lord. As Moses wrote, "And thou shalt set it before the Lord thy God" (Deuteronomy 26:10).

Your offering is transferred by the earthly priest to the hands of the High Priest.

In Old Testament times it was only the High Priest who could enter beyond the veil and there offer sacrifices to God.

Today, your gift goes from the minister who has been given the authority to hold the office, directly to our High Priest, Christ Jesus. The Lord then approaches the throne of God with what has been placed in His hand.

A priest can only present what those making the sacrifices have offered. He worships God with that tribute. "Here it is, Father," he says as he begins to worship.

Which Twin?

Years ago, a missionary told the story of a woman in a remote area of the Orient who gave birth to twins. "One baby was perfect," he observed. "The other had twisted limbs and was physically deformed."

The people worshipped a river god that flowed through their village.

"I wasn't sure what would take place," he said, "so I followed as she took the two infants down to the edge of the river and placed one of the newborn babies beside her."

He watched from a distance as she then lifted the other child up as if to offer it to a pagan god. He could hear the woman faintly saying something, but could not distinguish the words. "Then," he stated, "she quickly threw the child into the raging swirl of the swiftly moving river."

The missionary's heart was wrenched. He ran as quickly as he could to the woman, believing the deformed baby had been sacrificed to the gods.

"As I approached her," he recalled, "I was totally shocked. It wasn't the disfigured baby who had been thrown into the river, but the child who was beautiful and healthy. The crippled and deformed twin rested by the mother's side.

How could you do such a thing?
he asked the woman, who had tears
streaming down her cheeks. How could
you kill your child?

Then he added, "If you felt it necessary to sacrifice one of your children, why not choose the one who faced a difficult life, full of challenges and trials? Why have you kept this child and killed the baby that was healthy?"

135

The pagan woman replied, "That's the difference between you and us. We only offer the best to our gods."

Far too often, we keep for ourselves the best and offer to the Lord that which costs us little. Five percent is not ten percent. It may soothe a person's conscience, but it doesn't appease God.

We need to reflect on what the prophet Malachi wrote long ago. "Ye offer polluted bread upon mine altar; and ye say, Wherein have we polluted thee? In that ye say, 'The table of the Lord is contemptible'" (Malachi 1:7). We have polluted the sanctuary of a Holy God with soiled sacrifices.

The Lord says, "Go ahead and offer your desecrated offering, but I won't be listening to your songs, and I won't be hearing your prayers, for you have polluted my altar."

Scripture declares that "By faith Abel offered unto God a more excellent sacrifice than Cain" (Hebrews 11:4). Why? It was blood. It was obedience.

Give your best to God and prepare to see His abundance released into your life.

GOLDEN KEY #7

MIRACLE WORKING POWER OF THE SANCTIFIED SEED

You may never notice it on the surface, but there is something very special about the seed you present to God.

If you have earned $100 and bring a crisp, new $10 bill to the Lord as His tithe, it is not an ordinary piece of currency anymore than the rod of Moses was an ordinary stick or the mantle of Elijah was an ordinary piece of cloth. As we'll discover, it has miracle working power.

Here is an important verse the Holy Spirit allowed me to see. "Then thou shalt say before the Lord thy

God, I have brought away the hallowed things out of mine house" (Deuteronomy 26:13). And he presented those things to the Lord.

What are the "hallowed things?" They are specific items that have been sanctified, set apart, earmarked and anointed by God Himself. On each such designated article there is a sign that reads: "Do Not Touch!"

An Uphill March

One of my favorite stories in the Old Testament is that of Joshua and the battle of Jericho. I can visualize the army marching around the city seven times with the priests blowing their trumpets. On the final circle Joshua commanded the people, "Shout; for the Lord hath given you the city" (Joshua 6:16).

What happened? Immediately the walls of Jericho came tumbling down and the Israelites marched triumphantly into the city.

Joshua, and the thousands who were with him, rejoiced. Yet it was only the beginning.

The next target was the city of Ai — an uphill march of about fifteen miles from Jericho. First, a few of Joshua's men were sent to spy out the land.

They returned and reported, "No problem. Don't worry. Let most of the army rest. There are only a handful of men up there."

Joshua sent three thousand men to capture Ai — a

small contingent of his vast army. But they were in for a shock. Many of the invading troops were killed and the Israelites "fled before the men of Ai" (Joshua 7:4).

Joshua was humiliated. He tore his clothes and fell facedown before the ark of the Lord. He cried,

> *Would to God we had been content, and dwelt on the other side of Jordan!* (Joshua 7:7).

What went wrong? If God had promised victory, why were they so defeated?

Scripture tells us that "The children of Israel committed a trespass in the accursed thing" (Joshua 7:1). Other translations don't say "accursed," but an "anointed" or "sanctified" thing.

Here was the root of Joshua's difficulty. The Lord, knowing that there would be twenty-six more victorious campaigns ahead, told the leader to tell his men that when they captured Jericho, "all the silver, and gold, and vessels of brass and iron, are consecrated unto the Lord: they shall come into the treasury of the Lord" (Joshua 6:19).

God was taking His share in advance.

Since those things were sanctified, they would become cursed to anyone who would touch them. God said, "Keep yourselves from the accursed thing, lest ye make yourselves accursed" (v.18).

After the embarrassing defeat at Ai, God told Joshua, "Israel hath sinned . . . they have even taken of the accursed thing" (Joshua 7:11).

God instructed the leader it was time for the entire army to be consecrated and sanctified. The individual who had caused the problem simply had to be removed before they could ever fight again.

The next morning Joshua ordered that an inspection be made tribe by tribe, clan by clan, and family by family. When they questioned the tribe of Judah, Joshua singled out a man by the name of Achan and said, "Tell me now what thou hast done; hide it not from me" (v.19).

Immediately, Achan confessed that when he saw the Babylonian garments and all the gold and silver, he said, "I just had to have some of those things." He took a beautiful robe, two hundred shekles of silver and a wedge of gold.

Achan admitted, "I coveted them, and took them; and behold, they are hid in the earth in the midst of my tent" (v.21).

He lost everything — his family, his possessions and his life, because he touched what was sanctified.

The Agony of Defeat

Why were the Israelites defeated at Ai? Here are

three reasons:

1. They were all affected by the disobedience of one.

When just one person takes what belongs to God, thousands, even millions suffer. The Lord spoke through Malachi that the people had robbed God in tithes and offerings. He declared: "Ye are cursed with a curse; for ye have robbed me, even this whole nation" (Malachi 3:9).

This was a national sin. Oh, there were many in Israel who were paying God His tenth. But there were some who were not. You see, we are tied to one another. Your actions affect me. My actions affect you.

I believe the reason we've never seen the mighty revival God wants to send to this planet is because Christians are not obedient in their giving.

The moment that begins to occur, God is going to rend the heavens and unleash a great outpouring. I'm convinced of it.

When Christians across the land move into obedience, our entire nation will be transformed. God will look down from His holy habitation and grant blessing after blessing.

Right now we are losing the battle. We're losing against cancer, against doubt and distress, and against poverty. Even though Satan is a weaker opponent, he's defeating us, because we are not in obedience and unity.

In the words of the Psalmist, "Behold, how good and how pleasant it is for brethren to dwell together in unity!" (Psalm 133:1).

2. They were not operating at full strength.

Just because Ai was a smaller city than Jericho, it was no reason to reduce the size of the force. When you're up against an enemy, you need to operate at maximum efficiency.

Instead, Joshua listened to those who said, "We need some "R and R" — rest and recreation. And they suffered defeat.

3. The vision was not clearly communicated.

The battle of Jericho had been planned down to the smallest detail. Every man had his orders, and Joshua was in full control.

At Ai, victory was assumed, but there was no master plan. Sin had to be removed from the camp before God could continue His work.

When Achan confessed and had been permanently removed from the camp, Joshua sent thirty thousand of

142

his finest fighting men into Ai. This time they were victorious.

The Golden Goblets

Belshazzar, the king of Babylonia, threw a party for a thousand of his nobles. And while they were drinking he suddenly declared, "I want someone to go over to the house of God and bring us the golden goblets."

He should have known better. Those were the items that had been sanctified to the Almighty and were only to be used in the sanctuary of the Lord. They were made from the same gold and fashioned by the same goldsmiths as others he could have used, but these were special. They were dedicated and set apart only for the Lord.

When the goblets arrived, the drunken king lifted the glasses high and said, "Drink! Drink!" They "praised the gods of gold, and silver, of brass, of iron, of wood, and of stone" (Daniel 5:4).

God didn't wait to punish him. The Bible says, "In the same hour came forth fingers of a man's hand. and wrote . . . upon the plaster of the wall" (v.5).

Here were the words that were written:

Thou art weighed in the balances and art found wanting (Daniel 5:27).

Scripture records that the king turned pale, and he was so frightened that his knees knocked together and his legs buckled and gave way.

That night, like a flood, the armies of his enemies invaded the land and he was slain. His kingdom was divided and given to the Meads and the Persians.

Belshazzar died for no other reason than touching what he had no business touching. He was weighed by God's standards and was "found wanting."

Even though Belshazzar had material possessions, he lost it all because he took what belonged to God.

Those things that are sanctified and dedicated to the Lord take on a significance far greater than the physical elements they possess. The ark of the covenant was more than wood, cloth and precious stones. It was anointed by God, and even the earth on which it rested became hallowed ground.

God has absolute power because He is absolutely Holy — separated from everything else.

Why do I tell people that one dollar out of every ten is set apart by the Lord before it ever leaves your hand? Because tithing is a non-negotiable issue in God's kingdom. It's already earmarked by the Lord —

as if a corner tab has been folded down, or it contains an indelible mark of some kind. God declares, "That one is mine!"

If you take what belongs to the Lord and use it for some other purpose, it becomes unclean and unholy. Out of love and concern I am obligated to tell you that you curse your children by putting tennis shoes on their feet bought with God's tithe.

What is the Lord's belongs to Him alone.

Why did God ask us to bring Him the "hallowed things?" Because the heart, mind and power of the Lord is redemptive. He wants to redeem, sanctify and anoint what we place in His hands.

More Than Enough

Through the ages, the work of the Lord has always been to take us from where we are to the place He yearns for us to be. That's why He says, "I will sanctify a portion of your increase." By sanctifying it, He separates and releases it to have miracle-working power."

He not only wants to fill your cup, He wants it to run over. As the Psalmist wrote:

> "Yea, though I walk in the valley of the shadow of death,
> I will fear no evil: for thou art with me.

145

Thy rod and staff they comfort me.
Thou preparest a table before me in the pres-
ence of mine enemies.
Thou anointest my head with oil;
My cup runneth over.
Surely goodness and mercy shall follow me all
the days of my life:
And I will dwell in the house of the Lord
forever" (Psalm 23:4-6).

It's in Your Hand

Don't despise even the small things God presents to
you.

Do you remember what happened to Moses at the
Red Sea? The enemy had chased them into the water,
and they were about to drown.

"Stretch out that rod, Moses," someone called to
him.

"Oh, you mean this little stick of wood?" he
replied.

That rod was more than a branch from a tree that
had been whittled to fit his hand. It had been anointed
by God. And when Moses held it over the waters, they
miraculously parted. The children of Israel walked on
dry ground and were saved.

What do you have in your hand? You say, "Oh it's

nothing! Just a ten dollar bill. It can never pay the debts I owe."

Let me tell you a secret. When God touches that little piece of paper He can multiply it until a mountain of obligations disappear.

When you tithe, you are not just placing paper in a plate. When you send an offering, there is more than a check in that envelope. You are returning something to God as an act of faith and worship.

Stretch that sanctified seed over the distress of your life and watch the miracle begin. The Lord will part the waters of debt and distress. He will cause you to walk on dry ground.

GOLDEN KEY #8

SOW YOUR SEED IN TIME OF FAMINE

"What are you going to build out here?" a neighbor asked me while I was surveying a bare piece of land. He had seen me on the site and was curious to know what was going on.

"We're going to build a church," I told him.

"Well, how big is it going to be?" he continued inquisitively.

"It's going to seat just over five thousand people," I responded.

"Five thousand people?" he repeated. "Are you sure you need something that large?"

The man knew that we had a small building on a cornfield on a road nearby and walked away scratching

149

his head.

When the news media heard of our plans, they asked, "Don't you think it's rather dangerous to obligate your congregation to such a gigantic building program?" The artist's rendering of the project looked like a spaceship that had landed in an open field.

I smiled and said, "Just wait. You'll see what will happen on this property."

If I had been an astute businessman, or even a wealthy investor, I would have never undertaken such a risky venture.

I wasn't a conservative executive, however. I was a blood-bought, Spirit-filled, Bible-believing preacher whose mustard-seed faith had grown to the size of a mountain. When I looked at those plans I didn't see 5000 seats, I saw 5000 *people* with their hands raised toward heaven, worshipping the King of Kings.

Tilling the Soil

Golden Key number eight is essential if you plan to experience God's abundance: *Sow your seed in time of famine.*

Moses told the children of Israel that they were to set aside a tithe of everything they produced. It was for God, not for their own use. With a pure heart, they should be able to say to the Lord, "I have not eaten thereof in my mourning" (Deuteronomy 26:14).

The Spirit has also made those words plain to me.

When times are tough, that's not the moment to devour your seed. It's the time to plant it.

Years ago I met a man who was selling mutual funds, and I still remember his advice for building long term wealth. He said "Don't eat your seed." In other words, don't spend every dollar that comes your way. Plant a portion of it for tomorrow, and watch it begin to multiply.

That same principle has been practiced by successful farmers since the first field was cleared and the first crop was planted.

In ancient Israel, there was once a famine so great that Isaac was ready to flee to Egypt. There was no rain and the fields were bare. Nothing but dust and parched, dry ground.

But the Lord had another plan. He appeared to Isaac and said, "Dwell in the land which I shall tell thee of" (Genesis 26:2).

Following the Lord's command, he tilled the soil and planted his meager seed. Scripture records that "Isaac sowed in that land, and received in the same year an hundredfold: and the Lord blessed him" (Genesis 26:12).

151

Do you understand what it's like to get a one hundred percent increase? Isaac's income was <u>doubled.</u>

The abundance continued until he became extremely wealthy. "He had possession of flocks, and possession of herds, and great store of servants: and the Philistines envied him" (v.14).

Can you imagine the fate of Isaac if he had failed to listen to the voice of the Lord? He would never have known the reality of what God promised to his father, Abraham. The Lord said, "I will make thy seed to multiply as the stars of heaven, and will give unto thy seed all these countries; and in thy seed shall all the nations of the earth be blessed" (v.4).

Twenty Percent Interest

This may come as a surprise, but did you know that the Lord will give you permission to use His tithe for your personal needs in the time of a crisis? There's only one condition. You have to pay twenty percent interest on the money when you "settle up."

Here's what Moses told the people: "If a man will at all redeem ought of his tithes, he shall add thereto the fifth part thereof" (Leviticus 27:31).

So, if you're in a difficult spot and you feel it is

imperative to use the ten percent you've set aside for the Lord, you have the scriptural authority to do so. When it's time to pay it back, remember, add the twenty percent.

I shared this with a married couple who had recently become Christians. They shook their heads and said, "In our lifetime, we could never give the Lord what we owe Him — plus interest — for the years we didn't tithe." They asked,"What should we do?"

"First," I told them, "You must repent. Then you need to plead for mercy and grace regarding the ignorance that caused your past failings. God may wipe the record clean, but now that you have the light, He expects you to walk in it. No more excuses."

Causing Your Own Crisis

Some people don't wait for a real famine to develop. They create their own scarcity with a pessimistic attitude, a gloomy outlook and woeful words. They literally talk themselves into a crisis. I'm certain you've heard their whining:

"I just don't know how I'm going to make it."

"The forecast for our business doesn't look too promising."

"There seem to be a lot of people declaring bankruptcy these days. I sure hope I don't have to."

"I haven't been feeling too well lately. I wonder if it's something serious."

The law of sowing and reaping applies to much more than barley and rye. If you sow doubt, despair and defeat, that's exactly the crop you will harvest.

One of the most powerful verses in the Old Testament declares: "He that observeth the wind shall not sow; and he that regardeth the clouds shall not reap."(Ecclesiastes 11:4).

What happens to the worrywart who won't plant a crop? The outcome is really very simple. He will starve.

When you dwell on the wind instead of the Word, you're headed for disaster. That's exactly what Simon Peter discovered.

The disciples were together in a boat on the Sea of Galilee when a dangerous storm arose in the middle of the night. Suddenly, Jesus came to them — walking on the water.

When the disciples saw Him they were terrified. "It's a ghost!" they exclaimed.

Jesus immediately tried to calm their fear. Speaking through the storm, He said, "It is I; be not afraid" (Matthew 14:27).

Peter wasn't sure. He said, "Lord, if it be thou, bid me come unto thee on the water" (v.28).

Jesus said, "Come" and Peter got down out of the boat and walked on the water toward Jesus.

Then he made a big error. Scripture records that "When he saw the wind . . . he was afraid; and beginning to sink, he cried, saying, Lord save me" (v.30).

He took his eyes off of Christ, the living Word, and instead looked at the wind and was paralyzed with fear.

We Need Rain

Your situation may seem hopeless, but you serve a creative God who can cause streams to flow in the desert.

Once, when the armies of Israel set out to fight against Moab, the land was so barren in the wilderness of Edom that for seven days, "there was no water for the host, and for the cattle that followed them" (2 Kings 3:9).

The prophet Elisha came upon the scene and God gave him a directive. He announced: "Thus saith the Lord; Make this valley full of ditches" (2 Kings 3:16).

Can you imagine it? The people were crying, "Lord, we need rain. Our cattle are dying, and our grapes are withering on the vine. Lord, please, send rain."

In a dry valley that hadn't seen moisture for months, God told them to get out their shovels and start digging ditches.

Elisha said, "Wait a minute, Lord. Why should I break my back out there moving dirt? There are no clouds on the horizon. I hear no distant thunder. There's not even a breeze that could blow a cloud this direction if one came along. Why should I waste my time?"

The Lord spoke to Elisha and instructed him to declare to the people: "Ye shall not see wind, neither shall ye see rain; yet that valley shall be filled with water, that ye may drink, both ye, and your cattle" (v.17).

God was saying, "If you'll dig the ditch, I'll send the rain and irrigate your land. But first, you have to dig."

The God of supernatural abundance caused a flash flood in the mountains of Edom and "the country was filled with water" (v.20).

If what is in your hand is too small to be your harvest, determine to make it your seed.

When the cupboard is almost empty and the barrel of oil is down to the last drop, it's not a time to mourn.

All you need are a few tiny seeds and a great big shovel.

Start digging!

TEN GOLDEN KEYS TO YOUR ABUNDANCE

GOLDEN KEY #9

UNCLEAN SEED

Moses, in his instructions to the children of Israel, warned against using the tithe for any impure purpose. He said, "Neither have I taken away aught thereof for any unclean use" (Deuteronomy 26:14).

How can you expect to have a field of golden grain when you plant rows and rows of diseased, contaminated seed?

The person who sows in sin needs more than "weed and feed" to salvage a harvest. The root of the problem is much too deep for that.

Across the world there is a great deal of confusion regarding sin. People want to know:

- Is sin inherited, or is it acquired?
- Is sin unbelief?
- Is it rebellion?
- Is it perversity?
- Is it sensuality, or selfishness?

■ Is sin an outward act, or is it an inward thought or motive?

We know that because of Adam's fall in the Garden of Eden, we were born with a sinful nature that is only cleansed by the applied blood of Christ. But what about the transgressions we commit? As one man asked me, "Exactly when do my actions become sin?"

Look at the definition given by John. He declared, "Whosoever committeth sin transgresseth also the law: for sin is the transgression of the law" (1 John 3:4).

Sin is lawless — in other words, it is not a regulation or an ordinance. Instead, it is a deed.

It's not the absence of law, but the <u>breaking</u> of the law that produces iniquity. God sets a standard for our moral and physical behavior. It's a "mark" that we are measured against.

Missing that mark is the result of breaking God's law When that happens, it is sin.

We must play by the rules.

Paul wrote to Timothy that no one serving as a soldier should become involved in civilian affairs — if he wants to please his commanding officer (2 Timothy 2:4). Similarly, an athlete doesn't receive the winner's prize unless he competes according to the rules. Paul wrote, "If a man also strive for masteries, yet is he not crowned, except he strive lawfully" (2 Timothy 2:5).

What does this have to do with abundance? Everything.

As a direct result of failing to meet God's standard, what was once spotless and pure can become soiled and contaminated. You will find yourself sowing unclean seed that produces thorns and thistles instead of the bounty of the Lord's supernatural supply.

Isaiah wrote, "Touch no unclean thing . . . be ye clean, that bear the vessels of the Lord" (Isaiah 52:11).

God's mark is abundance. His measuring gauge always reads "full."

Three Questions

The tragedy of sowing unclean seed can be avoided. It begins with an understanding of the nature of sin, how it operates, and what it produces. Here are three vital questions we need to ask:

1. What is the *basis* of sin?

I grew up believing that lust was sin. But when I began to study God's Word I discovered that was not true.

Here's how James explains it. "But every man is tempted, when he is drawn away of his own lust, and enticed. Then when lust hath conceived, it bringeth forth sin: and sin, when it is finished, bringeth forth death. (James 1:14,15).

Have you ever desired something so passionately that nothing could keep you from it? Some people feel that way about a fishing trip, a new car, even a slice of apple pie at a favorite restaurant.

These things can cause more than an intense craving. They can produce lust.

Somehow we've associated that word only with evil, but it's not always true.

The apostle Paul lusted when he struggled with the question of life or death. He wrote: "For I am in a strait betwixt two, having a desire to depart, and to be with Christ, which is far better" (Philippians 1:23).

Jesus lusted when He told the disciples, "With desire I have desired to eat this passover with you" (Luke 22:15).

Far too often, things God meant for good have been used for evil. As Paul wrote: "I know, and am persuaded by the Lord Jesus, that there is nothing unclean of itself; but to him that esteemeth anything to be unclean, to him it is unclean" (Romans 14:14).

While lust is not sin, there is no iniquity that does not begin in lust, because it is the basis of sin.

162

The transgressions we commit don't just "happen." They are acts of our will.

Much too often, when an unmarried teenage girl becomes pregnant with the child of her boyfriend, they will say, "Well, we really didn't plan for this to happen. We were in a moment of passion and we couldn't help ourselves."

No. That's not true.

Anything you allow to happen has your permission. You don't simply "fall into it." It has your foreknowledge. It is planned.

Stop blaming Satan for what you willed to do. And please don't blame the Lord. I'll never forget hearing a girl in trouble announce, "Well, I can't help it if God gave me these emotions!"

As I once told a young man, "You'd better think twice before you start playing with fire. You can change your actions. If your mouth will work to kiss, it will work to talk."

What about someone who is forced to do something against his or her will — including rape or taking drugs? Have they sinned?

For example, you may abhor alcohol and have made a vow to God to never let it touch your lips. But what if four or five people held your mouth open and poured a pint of Jack Daniel's whiskey down your throat. The alcohol hit your bloodstream and you passed out.

Did you become drunk? Yes.

Did you sin? No.

2. What is the *method* of sin?

A man who is serving time in prison for selling child pornography, admitted that his perversion didn't begin overnight.

"At first," he said, "I looked at magazines with photos of nude women that had been 'airbrushed' to be less offensive." But he confessed that didn't satisfy. "So I started buying 'hard core' publications."

Still unsatisfied, he then turned to an interest in photos of nude men. "Finally," he said, "to appease my sexual urges I turned to lewd photos of children, and I got involved in a ring of people with the same obsession. That's why I'm here."

Sin's method is to seduce you into a polluted cesspool until you drown.

It happens through enticement.

James says, "Let no man say when he is tempted, I am tempted of God: for God cannot be tempted with evil neither tempteth he any man" (James 1:13). How does it happen? We are tempted when, by our own evil desire, we are pulled away and "enticed" (v.15).

We become hooked by sin in much the same way as fishermen and hunters catch their prey.

- It's the colorful lure that captivates the rainbow trout.
- It's the hand-carved decoy that attracts the wild ducks.
- It's the baited trap that catches the red-tailed fox.

Through life's journey, the devil of deceit will never stop enticing you. He says,

I can show you a shortcut to your destination. If you'll take this path you can get there much faster.

As a result of his lies, millions have been tempted by instant gratification, and their lives have been ruined.

God alone sets the boundaries within which we are to live. What happens inside that circle is lawful. Your wedding vow means that you have pledged to stay in the center of His will.

Don't be beguiled to cross the line and enter a world that is tarnished and stained.

3. What is the *result* of sin?

Iniquity not only separates us from God, but robs us of the abundant life He has planned.

Those who take what is pure and cause it to become polluted will never know peace. As the prophet Isaiah wrote, "The wicked are like the troubled sea, when it cannot rest, whose waters cast up mire and dirt (Isaiah 57:20).

What is the ultimate result of transgression? "Sin, when it is finished, bringeth forth death" (James 1:15).

Take a Close Look

Have you looked carefully at the seed you are sowing? Is it free of impurities? Will it produce a harvest you'll be proud to present to the Lord? Perhaps it's time for a close examination.

First: Examine your motive.

Some people do the right thing, but for the wrong reason. They fulfill the letter of the law, but not the spirit of the law.

Second: Examine your mandate.

The Lord will make His directions clear. If you give your seed for a use other than what He has commanded, it becomes unclean — no matter how worthy the recipient. For example, if the Lord tells you to help build a Bible school in Bosnia, yet you give the money to the local homeless shelter instead, your gift is tainted and doesn't carry God's blessing.

Third: Examine your manner.

It's not a sin to have wealth. The problem arises if we gain our riches in an immoral way. That's when the seed becomes defiled. Prosperity must occur within the framework of God's law.

Fourth: Examine the message.

Here's the best news of all. "If we confess our sins, he is faithful and just to forgive us our, sins and to cleanse us from all unrighteousness" (1 John 1:9).

Your unclean seed can be cleansed and made new!

TEN GOLDEN KEYS TO YOUR ABUNDANCE

GOLDEN KEY #10

GOD CAN'T BLESS WHAT HE'S CURSED

"Why would a God of love, joy and peace have so many rules and regulations?" a man from New York once asked me.

I returned the question by asking one of my own. "Have you ever played baseball or football?"

"Many times," he responded.

"Well," I continued, "were there any official rules you had to obey?"

"Of course there were," the man acknowledged.

I explained that without clear regulations it would be totally impossible to play any game. It would be chaos.

God designed this world with an order that is so precise scientists and astronomers have been trying to figure it out for centuries. He also gave clear directives for how He expects us to live.

> *The "do's and don'ts" of God's law are not for our chastisement, but for our safety, security and direction.*

Like any good father, God blesses us when we obey and corrects us when we stray.

If our disobedience becomes unacceptable, the Lord can take the drastic step of pronouncing a curse — either on an individual or some particular object.

He's done it many times.

The Great Warning

After Moses taught that God wants our seed to be sown in time of famine and not used for anything unclean, he said, "Neither . . . have I given ought thereof for the dead" (Deuteronomy 26:14).

In God's sight, giving to dead idols is cursed.

The apostle Paul repeated the warning in the New Testament. He said that our tithe was not to be offered to idols to honor those who had departed. Paul warned, "If any man say unto you, This is offered in sacrifice unto idols, eat not" (1 Corinthians 10:28).

Through the prophet Ezekiel, God gave a warning to those who would set up a stumbling block such as an idol. He declared, "I will set my face against that man . . . and I will cut him off from the midst of my people" (Ezekiel 14:8).

God can't bless what He has cursed, and you can't either.

Immediately following the great lesson God taught regarding our giving, the Lord told Moses that those who disobeyed would be cursed. There were twelve specific warnings:

1. Cursed is the man who carves an image or casts an idol (Deuteronomy 27:15).
2. Cursed is the man who dishonors his father or his mother (v.16).
3. Cursed is the man who moves his neighbor's boundary stone (v.17).
4. Cursed is the man who leads the blind astray on the road (v.18).
5. Cursed is the man who withholds justice from the alien, the fatherless or the widow (v.19).
6. Cursed is the man who sleeps with his father's wife (v.20).

7. Cursed is the man who has sexual relations with any animal (v.21).
8. Cursed is the man who sleeps with his sister (v.22).
9. Cursed is the man who sleeps with the mother of his wife (v.23).
10. Cursed is the man who kills his neighbor secretly (v.24).
11. Cursed is the man who accepts a bribe to kill an innocent person (v.25).
12. Cursed is the man who does not uphold the words of this law by carrying them out (v.26).

God still wasn't finished. He said, "If thou wilt not hearken unto the voice of the Lord thy God, to observe to do all his commandments and his statutes which I command thee this day; that all these curses shall come upon thee, and overtake thee" (Deuteronomy 28:15):

- Your basket and your kneading trough will be cursed (v.17).
- The fruit of your womb will be cursed (v.18).
- The crops of your land will be cursed (v.18).
- The calves of your herds and the lambs of your flocks will be cursed (v.19).
- You will be cursed when you come in and cursed when you go out (v.19).

172

Those words weren't spoken just to get our attention. God has always been concerned about our transgressions.

When we attempt to live contrary to the Word and attempt to touch what God has cursed, there is nowhere to turn.

> *It's been said that "God has no grandsons." Just because our parents and grandparents walked with the Lord, they can't protect us.*

We each must have a relationship with the Almighty.

Judgment for using what is cursed is inescapable. God said, "Though Noah, Daniel and Job were in it (communion with me), as I live, saith the Lord God, they shall deliver neither son nor daughter; they shall but deliver their own souls by their righteousness" (Ezekiel 14:20).

These great men of God could not even spare their own sons and daughters.

We can have the strongest prayer group in history, but it is impossible to overturn a decision already made by the Lord. If He has cursed something, we'd better not attempt to change it.

There is, however, one thing we can do. God

states: "Repent and turn yourselves from idols" (Ezekiel 14:6). The Lord is always pleading, "Please, come back to me."

It's Alive!

When God says, "Don't give your offerings to the dead," He means it. Our investment is to be in something that is vibrant and dynamic.

Here are four ways to know something is alive:

1. Living things have an appetite.

From my experience, it's not only *people* who are dead, but many ministries are, too.

Some churches have been in the same lifeless rut for longer than we can remember. They are completely satisfied to have "their little four and no more" sitting on a hillside talking to each other. They polish each others's armor and pretend everything is fine. Yet, it's not. They've lost their appetite, and they are much too close to the graveyard.

2. Living things take in and give out.

Do you know why the Dead Sea has its name? It takes water in, but it doesn't give any out. It's dead. On the other hand, the Sea of Galilee is healthy and alive, because it is open at both ends. The water freely flows.

It's not wise to be only a taker and not a giver.

3. Living things are never satisfied.

If you've ever been a mom or dad you know how quickly a tiny baby can cry for more milk. As we grow older, the desire for more never stops — it's only for different things. Striving is a sign of life.

4. Living things have growth.

We are serving a God of expansion and increase. That's why the Lord has given us the desire to reproduce. If a church or a ministry is not winning souls and expanding its horizons, I would think twice about investing in their mission.

A Greater Blessing

What a contrast between being average and being the best.

There have been thousands of professional baseball players in history. But if I asked you to name "the" baseball star of all time, you'd probably say, "Babe Ruth." If I asked you to name "the" greatest basketball player, you'd likely say, "Michael Jordan."

We not only need "a" blessing, we need "the" blessing.

According to Malachi, when we bring our tithe into the storehouse, God will pour out "a blessing." (Malachi 3:10). In Deuteronomy we learn about "the" blessing. It is a result of not only giving our tithe, but adding to it our offering.

Moses told the children of Israel to bring "your tithe . . . and your freewill offerings" to the house of the Lord (Deuteronomy 12:6). When that happens, "All these blessings shall come upon thee and over take thee" (Deuteronomy 28:2).

Here is what God promised to bless if we fully obey His commandments.

- The fruit of your womb (Deuteronomy 28:4).
- The crops of your land (v.4).
- The young of your livestock (v.4).
- Your basket and your kneading trough (v.5).
- You'll have victory over your enemies (v.7).
- Your barns and everything you put your hand to (v.8).

Our Creator's great desire is that you avoid the penalty of His curse. Here's the abundance He has promised: "The Lord shall make thee plenteous in goods, in the fruit of thy body, in the fruit of thy cattle, and in the fruit of thy ground" (v.11).

He will also give a financial blessing. "The Lord shall open unto thee his good treasure, the heaven to give the rain unto thy land in his season, and to bless all the work of thine hand" (v.12).

Even more, He will prepare for you a place of honor. "And the Lord shall make thee the head, and not the tail" (v.13).

The God of abundance I serve is not dead. He is alive and well.

I'm not being cursed, I'm being blessed!

IT'S TIME TO OPEN THE DOOR

You can possess all the keys in the world, but they will be of no value until three things happen:

First: You must place the key in the lock.
Second: You must turn the key.
Third: You must open the door.

The *Ten Golden Keys to Your Abundance* have been placed in your hands for a divine purpose. Jesus declared: "I will give unto you the keys of the kingdom of heaven" (Matthew 16:19).

He has entrusted them to your care, and now it is up to you.

I am praying you will not only open the door, but that you will absorb these truths until they become part of your spirit.

Here are the doors these Golden Keys will open:

Golden Key #1 will open the door to your inheritance.

Golden Key #1: The process of exchange.

Key Scripture: . . . when thou art come in unto the land which the Lord thy God giveth thee for an inheritance (Deuteronomy 26:1).

God wants you to exchange the bondage of your Egypt for the abundance of the Promised Land. Remember:

- When you let go of what *you* have, God will release what *He* has.
- It is vital that we exchange the world's kingdom for God's kingdom.
- The Lord can produce a change in your character and conduct.
- God desires prosperity for your soul, your mind and your body.
- The Lord will transform your income, your investments and your giving.
- God's laws of increase are better than man's.
- Exchange begins with repentance.
- Obedience is the door to abundance.

180

Golden Key #2 will open the door to your possession of the land.

Golden Key #2: The process of possession.

Key Scripture: You are to come into the land which the Lord thy God giveth thee for an inheritance and possessest it (Deuteronomy 26:1).

It is time to stand up to Satan and take back what is rightfully yours. God wants you to:

- Draw a line in the spiritual sand.
- Be transformed from a grasshopper to a giant-killer.
- Put on the whole armour of God (Ephesians 6:11).
- Know and trust His will.
- Stop relying on your feelings and start trusting His Word and His will.
- Use the combined power of faith, belief and prayer.
- Pray with fasting, intensity, authority, agreement and with the power of the Holy Spirit.
- Realize that abundance is given to help establish His kingdom.

Golden Key #3
will open the door to
safety and security.

Golden Key #3: The Process of protecting your seed.

Key Scripture: God's children not only came into the land of their inheritance and possessed it, but "dwellest therein" (Deuteronomy 26:1).

Your seed does not need to be devoured by the enemy. It is time to:

- Remember that God provides both possession and protection.
- Dwell on the land God has made available.
- Realize that God made both the mountains and the valleys, and that we must always rejoice.
- Defend your possession from the enemy.
- Know that the Lord is praying for you.
- Allow the Lord to be your refuge and fortress (Psalm 91).
- Never shy away from Satan.
- Remember the Lord's favor is contingent upon our action.
- Understand that God's long range plan is for your abundance.

Golden Key #4
will open the door to
a never-ending supply of water.

Golden Key #4: The process of watering your seed.

Key Scripture: After presenting their tithes and offerings, the people were instructed to say to the priest, 'I profess this day unto the Lord thy God, that I am come unto the country which the Lord sware unto our fathers for to give us' (Deuteronomy 26:3).

Remember, you are watering your seed when you:

- Make a profession of your faith.
- Recount your origin and your deliverance from bondage.
- Recount your persecution and how you came to possess the land.
- Thank God for His grace.
- Believe with your heart and confess with your mouth (Romans 10:8-10).
- Exercise your faith and combine it with action.
- See your situation as completed.
- Remember the water from the well of Jesus will never run dry (John 4:13,14).

Golden Key #5 will open the door to fertile soil.

Golden Key #5: The process of selecting your soil.

Key Scripture: Moses told the Children of Israel that when they came to the land God was giving, they should bring their first fruits unto the place which the Lord thy God shall choose to place his name there (Deuteronomy 26:2).

To find good soil, here is what to look for:

- Find a place where signs follow those who believe (Mark 16:17,18).
- Find a place where the Gospel is declared.
- Find a place where heaven, hell, the Cross, redemption through the blood, healing through the atonement and the second coming of Christ are preached.
- Find a place where Satan is being cast out (Mark 9:25).
- Find a place where healing is practiced (James 5:14).
- Find a place where Pentecost is alive and the gifts of the Spirit are at work.

Golden Key #6 will open the door to trust and obedience.

Golden Key #6: You must take your offering to the priest.

Key Scripture: And the priest shall take the basket out of thine hand, and set it down before the altar of the Lord thy God (Deuteronomy 26:4).

The Word clearly directs us to bring our first fruits to the house of God and present them to the priest. Remember:

- The world's resources have always belonged to God. It is His money before we ever give it.
- Accountability should be both in the pulpit and in the pew.
- We do not give *to* a priest but *through* a priest.
- In the fivefold ministry (Ephesians 4:11), each office has both authority and responsibility.
- Deacons and elders of the church must see their roles as ministries unto the Lord.
- Tithing is not optional; it is a direct order from our High Priest, Christ Jesus.
- The Lord requires obedience to His Word.

185

Golden Key #7
will open the door
to miracles.

Golden Key #7: Miracle-working power of the sanctified seed.

Key Scripture: Then thou shalt say before the Lord thy God, I have brought away the hallowed things out of mine house (Deuteronomy 26:13).

What we present to the Lord becomes sanctified and holy. Remember:

- The disobedience of one can affect everyone (Malachi 3:9).
- Joshua suffered defeat at Ai because someone had misused what was sacred (Joshua 7).
- Do not allow sin in the camp.
- Belshazzar lost everything because he took what belonged to God (Daniel 5).
- Do not touch God's tithe for your personal use.
- Give what the Lord has given you — regardless of its size.
- What is sanctified belongs only to God.
- Give as an act of faith and worship.

Golden Key #8 will open the door to your harvest.

Golden Key #8: Sow your seed in time of famine.

Key Scripture: I have not eaten thereof in my mourning (Deuteronomy 26:14).

When times are tough, that's not the moment to devour your seed. It's the time to plant. Never forget:

- Using God's money carries a hefty interest rate (Leviticus 27:31).
- Do not create your own lack through pessimism and gloom.
- If you sow doubt, despair and defeat, that is exactly the crop you will harvest.
- Dig your field and plant your crops, regardless of the circumstances.
- Do not look at the wind or the clouds (Ecclesiastes 11:4).
- The Lord will water your land with rain (2 Kings 3:17).
- If what is in your hand is too small to be your harvest, it is your seed.

Golden Key #9
will open the door
to what is clean and pure.

Golden Key #9: Unclean seed.

Key Scripture: Neither have I taken away ought thereof for any unclean use (Deuteronomy 26:14).

Moses warned against using the tithe for any impure purpose. Remember:

- God has established a mark that we are measured against.
- Always play by the rules. You cannot afford to break the laws of God.
- Failing to meet God's standards will result in contaminated seed.
- The basis of sin is willful lust.
- Always live within the boundaries God has set for you.
- Don't allow Satan to seduce you into a cesspool of sin.
- Never permit what is pure to become polluted.
- Examine yourself, your motive, your mandate, your manner and your message.

Golden Key #10
will open the door to abundance.

Golden Key 10: God can't bless what He's cursed.

Key verse: Neither . . . have I given ought thereof for the dead (Deuteronomy 26:14).

God has rules for the use of our seed. For example, Moses warned against giving to dead idols. Remember:

- Scripture lists those things that are cursed (Deuteronomy 27:15-26).
- God's decisions are final. If He has cursed something, we should not touch it.
- God commands that we give to ministries who are fulfilling the Great Commission (Mark 16:15)...alive with His work (v.17,18).
- Living things (1) have an appetite, (2) take in and give out, (3) are never satisfied and (4) are always growing.
- God has promised victory in every area (Deuteronomy 28:7,11,12).
- Abundance is promised to us when we fully obey His commandments (vv.4-8).

The Only Door

Are you ready for a miracle of abundance? There is only one door in which to place your key.

Jesus said, "I am the door: by me if any man enter in, he shall be saved, and shall go in and out, and find pasture" (John 10:9).

What does the Lord promise when we walk through the door? It is found in the very next verse. Jesus declares: "The thief cometh not, but for to steal, and to kill, and to destroy: I am come that they might have life, and that they might have it more abundantly (v.10).

I pray these *Ten Golden Keys to Your Abundance* will be released into your life — that they will unlock the door leading to your abundance.